John,

"Putting the real in it,

On behalf of

Richard Street

Gary K.

BALL OF
CONFUSION

RICHARD STREET
with GARY FLANIGAN

BALL OF CONFUSION
MY LIFE AS A TEMPTIN' TEMPTATION

TATE PUBLISHING
AND ENTERPRISES, LLC

Published by Tate Publishing & Enterprises, LLC
127 E. Trade Center Terrace | Mustang, Oklahoma 73064 USA
1.888.361.9473 | www.tatepublishing.com

Tate Publishing is committed to excellence in the publishing industry. The company reflects the philosophy established by the founders, based on Psalm 68:11,
"The Lord gave the word and great was the company of those who published it."

Published in the United States of America

ISBN: 978-1-62024-640-5
1. Biography & Autobiography / Composers & Musicians
14.05.02

ACKNOWLEDGMENTS

There are some very special people I must recognize. Beyond my life as a member of the Temptations, they are my soul and inspiration with respect to the music business. Without a doubt, they are my definition of "righteous brothers." I'm talking about my group members over the last ten years: Larry Johnson, Laurence Jones, Ed Watkins, Sean Brown, Terrence Forsythe, and Clayton Hooker. Together, under my name, we traveled the world from Spain to Tokyo, Africa to Ohio. And as a group, we never made our move too soon, but always on time.

Similarly significant, an honorable mention is certainly entitled my good friend Ron Tyson. Ron joined me in 1983 as a member of the Temptations, and at the writing of this book, he's still with the Temptations. As an individual, Ron has never lost his swagger.

Then there's my brother Daryl Street and his wife, Rosa, along with my sister-in-law, Edna Jue. Where would a brotha be without a brother and sisters like Daryl, Rosa, and Edna?

With continued respect to family, props are definitely due my wife Cindy's four children: Christine, Ed, Mark, and Charlyn. And my four children: Richard Street Jr., Brandi Street, Januari Street, and Brandon Street. Yes, it's a family affair, where all in the family are all the family that matters.

With that thought in mind, a father figure to me and a whole bunch of others is Berry Gordy Jr. Unquestionably, without Berry, the birth of my career as I know it today may have never been. Berry was the man with the plan who made it all happen.

Finally, there's Cindy. Through the timeless words of the Shirelles, something old, new, borrowed, and blue. Let me just say with regard to my life, my wife, the timely writing of this book:

"This is dedicated to the one I love."
While I'm far away from you, my baby,
I know it's hard for you, my baby,
Because it's hard for me, my baby,
And the darkest hour is just before dawn.
So, each night before you go to bed, my baby,
Whisper a little prayer for me, my baby,
And tell all the stars above,
"This is dedicated to the one I love."
Life can never be exactly like we want it to be.
But I can be satisfied just knowing you love me.
There's one thing I want you to do especially for me.
And it's something that everybody needs.
So, each night before you go to bed, my baby,
Whisper a little prayer for me, my baby,
And tell all the stars above,
This is dedicated to the one I love."

FOREWORD

It was a May Day in 1998. I was at my desk at John Marshall Law School in Atlanta, Georgia. On the phone was a guy who said he sang with the Temptations. I didn't catch his name; I only heard the Temptations.

Working at a law school as an adjunct professor of entertainment law, I was skeptical. After all, doing what I did at the time, when you're on the phone with someone claiming to be someone, there's only a couple things you can say and do.

Of course, the first thing I said is simply, "Yeah right," and hang up.

The second, of course, is to simply say, "Prove it," and quietly listen. Obviously, since you're reading this book, I chose the latter. I listened.

"Heard some talk about Papa doing some storefront preachin'. Talkin' about saving souls and all the time leechin'. Dealing in dirt and stealing in the name of the Lord. Mama just hung her head and said," was the flawlessly sung reply.

Well, being a Temptation fan, when I heard that verse from "Papa Was a Rollin' Stone" sung in exact duplicate fashion of what had been etched into my memory banks for the past twenty-six years, that was proof enough.

"What was your name again?" I said.

"Oh, now I've got your attention," the voice on the phone chuckled.

That day in May was the beginning of my friendship with Richard Street. In a prophetic way, that introductory telephone exchange between me and Richard kinda sets the stage for all you are about read.

I had been singing "Papa Was a Rollin' Stone" since it was first released in 1972. Yet I didn't know the name behind one of the voices that helped make the song all that it was, and more. I had asked Richard Street to prove himself. I had been singing Temptations' songs for more than half of my life. And here I am asking a Grammy Award winner to prove himself to me. Needless to say, I apologized profusely.

But Richard is cool. He didn't say, "Who are you to be quizzin' me?" He only said, "No problem, young man. There are sharks and charlatans out here. I wouldn't expect or respect anything less."

That's what I admirably respect about Richard Street. His coolness isn't cliché. Richard doesn't say what he doesn't mean. His words export strength of character that gives the doer and the hearer either encouragement or sudden pause. So when Richard said it was all good, I could keep it moving with confidence that it is what it is—no less and no more.

Richard Street reached out to me in 1998 because he was seeking a writer to work with him and former Temptation Ali Woodson on a motion picture film concept. Now, it was my turn to flip the script. I asked Richard, "Who am I that you would knock on my door?"

Richard replied in his characteristic keeping-it-real tone, "You don't know who you are, brotha?"

But I was saying, "Come on, man, why me? You are a Temptation. You can call anyone of a 1,001 folks you've crossed paths with over the years to get a writer to work on a movie about the Temptations."

Richard's reply was, "We hear you're a good writer. And since you don't have any Hollywood credits, that means we can afford you."

Well, here again, that's what I admire about Richard. He is a straight street. Nothing like that crooked one (Lombard) in San Francisco. In so many words and with no uncertain terms, I was told from jump street (pun intended) that I was being called because there was a need for a good and cheap screenplay writer.

Now, how many guys are smooth enough to tell another brotha, one who just happens to be a law school professor, that they need a "cheap" laborer, and it's received as a compliment rather than as an insult?

In my psychedelic defense, however, the fact that I was a Temptation fan went a long way toward my positive reception of the proposition. But, once again, here again is a testament to the strength of character that is found in honesty. No games, no smoke, no mirrors, and no tricks up the sleeve. Just the simple capability to come correct or not step at all in your direction is the approach of Richard Street.

You may have noticed that my references to Richard are not in the past tense. In some African cultures, there is a concept called *sasha*. It is the term for ancestral spirits that are known by someone still alive. There is also the concept called *zamani*, which is the term for ancestral spirits that are not known by anyone currently alive.

Sasha is concerned with the present time, the recent past, and the near future, while zamani is the limitless past. The sashas are the recently departed. Their time overlaps with people who are still alive on earth. In a way, according to African culture, the sashas are the living dead. They are not wholly or totally dead because they live on in the memories of the living.

Only when the last person knows that an ancestor dies will the ancestor leave the sasha to then become a zamani—the dead.

Breaking it down and putting the real in it (as Richard would often say), sasha and zamani are not stages of death; they are ontological dimensions of history.

Okay, *ontological* is a fifty-cent word that 50 Cent probably wouldn't use. But look the word up anyway. It's deep. In a way, *ontological* (ontology) "puts the real" in what Shakespeare was saying when Hamlet said, "To be, or not to be, that is the question."

Shakespeare was only being ontological. The real question being questioned was all about one's internal, external, and eternal existence. Like I said, it's deep.

So, referring to Richard Street in the past tense is a psychosocial challenge for anyone who sings any one of the Temptations' tunes.

In terms of an African culture, expressed as sasha, if you know a Temptations' song, you know Richard Street. That means "ontologically" speaking, you know Richard internally, externally, and eternally.

In terms of a global culture, expressed as YouTube, only when the last person alive knowing a Temptations' song dies will David Ruffin, Eddie Kendricks, Paul Williams, Melvin Franklin, Ali Woodson, Damon Harris, and now Richard Street really be gone and forgotten.

It simply is what it is, as long as we are and continue to be.

—Gary F. Flanigan

INTRODUCTION

In the beginning God created the heaven and the earth. And the earth became void, and darkness was upon the face of the deep. A ball of confusion?

My story as a Temptation is a lot like the book from which those opening lines are taken. On the street where I lived there was an Adam and Eve, a David and Goliath, a Martha and Mary, a Cain and Abel, a Sodom and Gomorrah, a Samson and Delilah, a Moses, a devil, a savior, a god, a heaven, and, of course, there was a hell.

Now, in the beginning, it was not my intention to write a book, but I also wanted to do a movie. I wanted to do a blockbuster that told the truth. The truth I wanted to tell wasn't a fairy tale, but it wasn't a Freddy Kruger either. It was about all the places that long and winding road took the temptin' Temptations.

There were the speed bumps along the way. And there was also that HOV lane where hitting 160 miles per hour was as routine as sunshine on a cloudy day. Being a Temptation meant you had to take risks—some calculated, some not. The word *temptation* itself suggests risk. If there wasn't a risk suggested in the very nature of the word *temptation*, would it really be a temptation?

Even though hitting one hundred on a rain-soaked highway of a day wasn't advisable, but more times than not, that was the advice us Temptations were being given by the likes of self as well as others.

So the problem with my movie idea was the fact that it takes quite a bit of money. And usually when there's a lot of money, there are a whole lot of others involved. Subsequently, a book is a lot more manageable.

I do believe it was my man Solomon (not Burke) who said, "Of making many books there is no end." After all, Smokey did do his book. Mary Wells and Wilson did theirs. And so did Otis (not Redding). So any'mo of Motown might be considered entirely too much or too little "Richard" penmanship for any soul to stand.

But as Marvin once upon a time so melodiously put it, "if the Spirit moves you?"

Well, I was moved. Just as the Bible says, "The Spirit of God moved upon the face of the waters" (which were deep). And that very same Spirit moved me. And I'm still motivated by that very same Spirit to get off into some deep revelations. I'm talking about some spiritual mysteries that will hopefully keep others from falling prey to temptations. That's temptations of a nonsinging variety.

But my story is not told to impress or depress. It's not about a biblical Job and what it is to suffer. It's simply about a job (as in employment) of biblical proportions. If you were a young adult in the mid 1960s or '70s, you know exactly what I'm talking about. Being a Temptation was "heavenly."

Indeed, we were the idols of many. Our fans treated us like modern-day Greek gods. I mean Mt. Olympus didn't have anything on Detroit's Motown. David Ruffin was an Apollo. Eddie Kendricks, Mercury. Melvin Franklin (with that deep voice), Neptune. Since Berry Gordy made it all happen, unquestionably, Zeus. And then there was me: Richard Street. Hercules (so I thought)!

If Motown was the "sound of young America" during that era, the Temptations were the eardrum. Whether you lived down in the valley or upon a hill, you knew "my girl" lived in a "psychedelic shack." And just because "beauty's only skin deep," you could care less if hers or your "papa was a rollin' stone."

Music defined the vocabulary of a Pepsi generation, and Motown had replaced Webster as the country's lexicographer and poet laureate.

In reflection, my life as a Temptation was full of them (temptations) because I was full of me. Therefore, my story as a Tempt is about a self-willingness to be led up into the wilderness to be tempted by the devil. It's about that devil showing me "all the kingdoms of the world and the glory of them" and saying, "All these things will I give you, Richard, if thou wilt sign right here on the dotted line."

But unlike Jesus who said, "Satan, get to steppin'," this greatest story I never told (until now) is about me and a bunch of others saying, "Do you want my middle initial too?"

Definitely, there is a spiritual connection in the true story of the temptin' Temptations that has never been told on film or in print because truth itself is spiritually connected. Truth is about growth. Since Jesus said, "Ye shall know the truth, and the truth shall make you free," how can you be made free if you don't grow?

Unfortunately, a lot of the books that have been written about the Motown era stifle the reader's spiritual growth. Yes, there were temptations in the spiritual sense of the Word. But there were also the triumphs in the same spiritual sense that have yet to be heard.

Let's put the real in it? How much spiritual growth is there to be found in you personally knowing who was doing drugs? Or who was doing who?

In the final analysis, does knowledge of who, what, when, where, and how an individual "slipped into darkness" lead you into the light?

The story I'm here to tell is not about feeding the hunger for gossip. Neither is it meant to scratch the itching ear of that inquiring mind that wants to know the dirty lowdown some fifty years after the fact. If you are looking for titillation, keep on truckin', baby. There's no tit for tat to suck on here.

The story of my life as a Temptation is about succeeding despite temptations, obstacles, impediments, failings, shortcomings, circumstances, challenges, and mess in all its assorted colors, shapes, and sizes. It's about making it to the top on the rough side of the mountain even despite your own self.

So again, if you're looking to find something else on the pages of this book, better try the neighborhood drugstore on the same block as that sex shop. Street life from my perspective is not about the vice; it's about the advice. It's about family—the good, the bad, and the ugly that had an innovatively creative way of making lemonade out of onions.

Just check out the spiritual symbolism that's found in such names as Supremes, Miracles, Wonder, Martha and Mary, Paul, and, of course, Temptations. There was even a Motown record label called Soul.

Can it really get any deeper than that in a spiritual sense of the Word?

Yes, just like the Bible doesn't tell you only about the good, this book right here doesn't tell you only about the bad. Contrary to the song "Ball of Confusion" and what you probably thought, my story is entitled the same because I had myself a ball. As a matter of fact, I think all twelve of us Temptations did. (Even I stopped counting after the first dozen!)

Just like spinning around on an amusement park ride, sooner or later you gots to get off. And when you do, that's when the spinning ain't too cool. Once you try to walk straight and your head is still trippin', that's when the ball gets confusing.

Unfortunately, a lot of folks got the "Ball of Confusion" title of that hit single twisted—a double entendre let's say. The "ball" as it was, was not only planet Earth. It was also planet Hollywood as in swingers. We were ballin' as Temptations. We were big ballers and shot callers. We were the original American Idols. The four judges were the four continents: the Americas, Africa, Asia, and Australia (all As being our grade). And if global warming had been as prevalent back there in that day, add Antarctica to the mix for an A+. Certainly, every snow-covered outpost with radio reception, as far as the South Pole, would have been exposed to a Temptations' tune.

Yes, we had a ball.

But just as the Bible says, "Remember Lot's wife," I say, "Remember Cinderella?" Lest we forget, Cinderella partied till the midnight hour. And instead of leaving with her, a whole lot of us "Cinderfellas" just stood around and watched homegirl run clean out of her shoes. Moral of the story, sometimes, you got to watch the ticktock too. Personally know what time it is in terms of your own personal life. Be able to make a few minor or major adjustments. Or simply modify the program if you really intend to hang, and not get hung.

So I'm not here to tell you something you already know because you've either seen or read it someplace else. My mission is to tell you something you think you know because you heard it somewhere else, but the facts of the matter were not all the way true.

For example, take the word *therapist*. Depending upon how you look at the facts, that's a word that can either describe your best friend or your worst enemy. Your counselor can very easily become "the rapist."

It's all about the tint of the shades you choose to view life through. When looking through a mirror darkly as pointed out in 1 Corinthians 13:12, sometimes the only thing you see is a reflection of yourself and the shadowy images behind.

The sho'nuff for real story of the temptin' Temptations is a modern-day parable with rhyme and reason. It cannot be camouflaged by the mirage of individual stories that play to the rhyme without explaining the reason.

Ball of Confusion: My Life as a Temptin' Temptation is a passion play of biblical proportions for all who felt the spirit of music made flesh through the rhythm and the blues of the body, mind, and soul.

THE THIRD OF SEPTEMBER

It was a day I'll always remember. No, my daddy didn't die physically. His death was a spiritual thing. He walked out on the family.

Yeah, just like the song, he left my mother, brother Robert, and me. The Adam of my life left the ponderosa shortly after I learned to walk.

There was a whole lot of bitterness between my mom and pop. If there had been an Oprah back there in that day, Cadell and Marguerite Street would have been sitting in the first row. Our house was dysfunctional spelled with all caps. And given the fact that my papa was a postal worker too! Well, you know we had it goin' on 24-7-365. Wally and Beaver Cleaver, me and my brother Robert weren't!

But I used to wonder how Wally and the Beaver would have turned out if their old man had worked for the post office. Ward probably would have been in one.

Anyway, the year was 1945. The place was Detroit, Michigan. I was three. And we were bankrupt even though the city then wasn't. It was also the day I first found out about "the move."

Of course, you realize during that World War II time that there just wasn't a day care on every corner. Being black and "Rich" in name only didn't necessarily mean acquaintanceship with a TV-land nanny type. The "hard-time Mississippi" that

Stevie talks about had nothing on the hard-time Michigan that my mom had to deal with.

As a small boy, I vividly remember the alarm clock ringing every morning at five sharp. Rain, sleet, or snow, my mother had a six thirty bus to catch to keep a roof over our heads and food in our stomachs. When I reminisce regarding my dearly beloved mom, her heart of gold was our rock of Gibraltar. So being West Virginny bound meant carrying as much of that rock as my small hands could hold.

First and foremost, "have faith in God" and "reach for your own goals so that other people will not take advantage of you." That's what my mama said. I guess that "piece of the rock" got embedded deep within my heart and soul. Certainly, it helped me overcome the reality of "a rollin' stone papa."

Don't let anybody tell you that environment doesn't shape behavior. If you grow up in the sticks, only a whole lot of determination keeps you from getting stuck.

Now, I know that these kinds of "hard-time" stories are not unique to "my street." There are a million and one stories in that naked city. So my relating all the above is not a stab at some poorer-than-thou portrayal. I was a kid in Detroit. And being a kid in Detroit is like being a kid anywhere in Soulsville. I saw the world with that "child's heart" Stevie Wonder also sang about.

True, looking back over the years, we all shed some tears. But we had to let it go. If we hadn't, it would have definitely been just another TKO, the kind Teddy sang about.

So here I am, now, some six decades and three thousand miles removed from Detroit, and folks are still talking about the motor city being on the verge of collapse. Few realize, or want to realize, when you live on the other side of the tracks (Soulsville), you're always on the verge of something.

Whether it's 1945 Detroit or 2001, the space odyssey is the fact that whatever space you're living in, you're probably only two missed paychecks away from being homeless and/or carless even in a city where cars are made.

Detroit way back in the day is not all that different from Detroit way up here in the now. It's just a matter of Mo' better media coverage now than it was back then. Facebook can put a face on who's who, as well as who ain't doing what they're supposed to do.

I mean, in 1945, if you were running for president, you could get in a smoke-filled backroom and say, "Let Detroit [Soulsville] go down the toilet." But when you're living in an age where everybody is packing a cell phone with a camera, unless you are incredibly stupid, you're going to check your mouth at the door along with your coat.

But in the class of '45, I didn't fully realize the depth and degree of political stupidity and racism that created the challenges faced by my mother. In her lone struggle to provide for me and my brother, we had food on the table, clothes on our back, shoes on our feet that fit, and new toys to play with on the first day of every Christmas.

Understand, in our house there was none of that twelve-days-of-Christmas stuff. If the fat man in the red suit didn't arrive by seven Christmas morning, the boyz in my hood knew you were SOL (so outta luck).

So given the fact that the street where we lived always seemed to have it going on, what more could two little boys ask for during the fall, winter, spring, and summer of 1945?

This brief insight into my genesis only serves to provide a future frame of reference. Sometimes there's a need to know where somebody has been if you are seriously interested in knowing how they happen to be where you find them.

The personal mind-set that led me into the Temptations was fashioned by the reality of being economically handicapped and not really knowing it. I'm talking about that "not having a pot to piss in or window to throw it out" mind-set that keeps you hanging on like the advice given in a Supremes' song.

There has to be something bigger than you that helps you make-believe that your house is a mansion when it's really a two-bedroom flat. Or maybe it's that philosophical outlook that denies the reality that you've been financially limited all of your "trying to make it real compared to what or that over there" life!

Yes, God bless the child that's got his own. But better yet, blessed is the child who has the revelation to get his own while he is still a youth. Because for those dudes who one day wake up like my man Rip Van Winkle, the only thing that they can do is say, "Dadgumit."

With determination, I decided I was not going to be like Rip. Rip got ripped off by his own hands. He was a willing participant in his own oppression because, for whatever reason, he laid himself down and did nothing to better or improve his condition. He slept for twenty years. Rewind your own life by twenty years and hit Delete. Look at what you've missed. *Dadgumit* probably won't be your choice of word!

My mind was made up early on. And with the realization that it was the blood, sweat, and tears of my mother who put food on the table, clothes on my back, shoes on my feet that fit, and gifts under the tree, I was not willing to let her down.

Yes, I was now ten years old with a brand-new sense of self! And I wasn't going to punk out like my old man. And I certainly wasn't going to keep my family hanging on to a tune that wasn't supreme. I was fully prepared to accept the role as man of my house.

You see, it wasn't called being a "dead-beat dad" back in that day. It was called getting your butt kicked by your very own son if you messed with "Eve," the mother of your life. That's what "playing the dozens" was about. The "yo, mama" thing was kind of a safety valve to let off steam. Rather than disrespect, yo mama was your everything!

When Eddie Kendricks sang, "You surely must know magic girl, cause you changed my life. It was dull an ordinary; you made it sunny and bright. I was blessed the day I found you. I'm gonna build my whole world around you. You're everything good girl and you're all that matters to me," the message being sent has a double meaning. Yo mama also knew magic if she was any kind of a mother.

In my day and in my neighborhood, the only social worker was a fist (or something more potent) upside your head if you weren't about the business of taking care of "your everything," who more than likely was your mother!

And when it came to social networking, back then it was calling someone to help if your fist wasn't big enough to make either a fitting or lasting impression!

Yes, sir, I was ten going on fifteen and talking serious smack to anybody who would listen. I was standing on my name (as in street), philosophizing with the fellas. And in Detroit, Michigan, many of the fellas I was on the corner with were fifteen going on twenty-five!

Being fatherless, you know I was picking up plenty information, taking names and numbers while simultaneously handing out receipts. I guess this is why folks back then seemed to be so much older than today's contemporary counterparts.

Here and now, when you see Marvin, Smokey, David Ruffin, Eddie Kendricks, Otis Redding, or Sam Cooke performing on YouTube old film clips from *American Bandstand, Shindig!,* or *Hullabaloo,* people don't realize that those guys were just barely beyond being teenagers!

There was none of that Boyz II Men stuff back then. When you got to the Apollo, you were a man. *Boy* wasn't even part of the vocabulary. If somebody called you boy, the proper response was, "You must have said Roy!"

That's why our masculinity and maturity was seen, heard, and felt in our music. The lyrics written, the music played, the songs sung were complete expressions of all five senses plus. I'm talking about the plus being the X factor that can only be described as ESP—extrasoul perception.

Don't just listen to the music! Look at the names parenthetically placed beneath those song titles! Holland-Dozier-Holland. Norman Whitfield. Smokey Robinson. Barrett Strong. Marvin Gaye. Stevie Wonder. They all have ESP! How do you explain somebody's ability to write a three-minute tune that is so tight that it not only touches your heart, but becomes embedded in your soul for a lifetime? That is power!

When Jesus said, "The words that I speak unto you, they are spirit, and they are life," he is talking about a power that few people really, really, really understand.

Other than the obvious, the power being divinely talked about is the spiritual significance of words. If it's positive words you're hearing, it's all about life. If your ears are waxed with bull crap, it's all about death.

For example, take the concept of having soul, being a soul sister or soul brother. "Having soul" means you can feel the vibe of the beat. It means you are in sync with the rhythm of the day and the night.

If you have no soul, it is impossible to feel the beat. And we all know what the deal is anytime a doctor lays hands on you and he or she can't feel the beat!

So you explain your ability to sing a Motown sound today just as fluently as you sang it twenty some years ago. Thirty-something years ago. Or how about forty!

But for some reason, a poem by Robert Frost, Henry W. Longfellow, or Jack Spratt just doesn't hang with you like that! This is why sweet soul music is soul music. It's way bigger than rhythm! And it's far better than blues!

Perhaps we were able to sing about love so well because our souls carried a man's appreciation for a woman. We had the realization that God created all women to be some Adam's very own Eve. No matter how fine or how ugggly a man or woman you happened to be, there was somebody out there for you. And the songs we sang gave everybody the hope of one day finding their very own soul mate by rhythmically tapping the soles of their shoes.

Remember the Percy Sledge song "When a Man Loves a Woman"? Percy may have looked like he was fifty-five, but my man was in his early twenties. I bet you can't even imagine a song like that being professionally cut by a twenty-something-year-old today?

Taking nothing artistically away from the television *American Idol* contestants I've seen over the past few years, they were simply not audiovisually believable singing the songs that dealt with the man-woman relationships that were described in the songs we sung when we were their biological age.

You have to be an old soul at a young age to sing "Me and Mrs. Jones" in the manner Billy Paul was able to do. And when Otis Redding said, "Try a little tenderness," he had to bring it—not just sing it.

Instead of songs being sung about a man loving a woman, many songs are presently sung about a woman being loved like she was a material possession whether she is a material girl or not. A *The Temptations Sing Smokey* tune would never refer to a woman as a car. When Smokey penned a song for us as Temptations to sing, it was all about celebration, not denigration.

The lines below are an example:

> You've got a smile so bright
> You know you could have been a candle
> I'm holding you so tight
> You know you could have been a handle

The way you swept me off my feet
You know you could have been a broom
The way you smelled so sweet,
you know you could have been some perfume

As pretty as you are, you know you could have
been a flower
If good looks was a minute
You know that you could be an hour

The way you stole my heart
You know you could have been a cool crook
And, baby, you're so smart
You know you could have been a schoolbook

Well, you could have been anything that you wanted to
And I can tell, the way you do the things you do.

Whether it was the Motown sound, the Philly sound, the Memphis sound, or James Brown getting down, us fellas knew exactly what Aretha meant when she dropped those seven letters on the ears of the world: R-E-S-P-E-C-T!

Even though my papa "rolled" out of our life, neither my brother nor I rolled with him. We were both Abel. But we stuck by our mother Eve. So in addition to my mind-set and frame of reference, I also had an attitude that was artistically molded by the very air that I breathed. After all, it's very difficult to listen to the songs we sung day in and day out and not be positively uplifted and influenced.

My mother, like 1,001 others, drew her strength from God and the music she heard. And by seeing my mom, she must not only survive but also thrive; her positive and unselfish spirit gave our home just as much peace and serenity as a church.

What we had then that few have now is that extended family support system. Yeah, my papa was a rollin' stone, but just like there are many fish in the sea, there are a whole lot of rocks on an unpaved road. There were father figures on the street where I lived. Granted, a father living in the home is far better than one on the outside looking in. But then and again, one on the outside looking in is far better than no one looking at all.

Our ability to triumph over temptation as kids was a direct result of the fact that there were grown men in the neighborhood who had our back as well as our young butts. An uncle, a grandfather, a cousin, or just that Fred Sanford–styled dude next door made it their individual and collective responsibility to be about the business of "good-lookin' out."

If any one of us boyz 'n the hood got out of line or for some inexplicable reason came down with a bad case of crazy-as-hellitis, our individual mothers knew all about it before the evening sun set on our individual humble abodes. Mama didn't take that mess. Nobody in the neighborhood took that mess. And because we knew it, we didn't individually or collectively play that mess.

But, of course, there were some who wanted to try their mama and their neighborhood "junkman" just for the hell of it. But, of course, to no one's surprise, that kind of game only played to an audience of one. The one being him or her who found him or herself being shipped off to something called reform school courtesy of the state.

Consequently, it just made more sense to do like a Nat King Cole–styled "Straighten Up and Fly Right."

Translated, there were "papas" on the block who weren't rollin' stones. And if you were a boy, there was a papa somewhere watching who was more than capable of cooling you out if you wouldn't, or your mama just couldn't.

Becoming old enough to understand the real deal along with having a genuine unselfish appreciation for the sacrifices made by my mother and others gave me some semblance of balance. It gave me my *soul*.

I didn't become a member of Motown's Temptations in a historical vacuum. I didn't wake up one morning with the psychological, sociological, and emotional maturity to be a member of one of the most famous and popular singing groups that the world has ever known. The preparation for success doesn't begin after you are successful.

It's written, "In the world ye shall have tribulation." You might not be able to fully prepare for the tribulation. You can, however, lay the foundation of preparation for the triumphs, be they great or small. My triumphs as an adult are the summation of my tribulations as a kid growing up on the street where I lived.

Yes, "it was the third of September. A day I'll always remember."

CRYING IN THE WILDERNESS

Who's your best friend?

MFSBs don't count. That's mothers, fathers, sisters, and brothers. Some of you old-schoolers knew that because you remembered the group! Four-footed best friends are also excluded.

Now, if you have someone you consider to be the best friend you've got, or ever had, reflect on how you met. Best friends that are truly best friends are truly a gift from God.

Melvin Franklin was my best friend. We went back to the third grade. And if you're more than twenty years old and have someone you've been partners with since you were eight, you just might be in line for *Guinness* book contention. Right along with me!

Melvin, of course, was an original Temptation. He was also known as David English. But just in case you don't recognize either name, certainly you'd recognize the voice. He was the guy with the deep bass voice. Actually, his voice was deeper than Barry White's, whose name many of you may more readily recognize.

Melvin came north to Detroit from Alabama. If somebody on the outside looking in saw my family and me as poor, they saw Melvin's condition indescribable. I mean there is poor. And then there is "*po*" without the "*or*."

How impoverished were the Franklins? Well, in order to make ends meet, the job Melvin had at the age of eight was to walk blind people (every day) up and down the streets. And, naturally, it was Melvin's job to hold and carry the tin cup. Yes, indescribable.

Needless to say, Melvin always got picked on by the kids and talked about by the adults. Most folks cannot even begin to imagine the embarrassment and humiliation this eight-year-old youngster felt. Having such an occupation, Melvin's self-esteem was so low; he had to look up to see the bottom.

The day Melvin and I first met, I remember it very well. Melvin; his brother, Jiggs; and his two sisters, Tootsie and Audrey, were sitting on the porch of their house as I walked down the street. Since Melvin and I were the same age, we noticed each other immediately and started talking. And strangely enough, the more we talked, the sooner we realized we were, in fact, distant cousins!

Again, here is that spiritual connection—God having hold of a situation as small and simple as two little boys meeting. What are the chances that two eight-year-old cousins from two different parts of the country would meet in the manner that we met? Two little boys who would eventually grow up to be intimately affiliated with one of the most popular singing groups of all time!

Call it coincidence. Call it chance. Call it strange. Call it weird. Call it whatever you will, because I call it amazing.

In the process of time, Melvin and I became as close as any naturally born brothers. In a spiritual sense, we were brothers. But in actuality, the reality found our discovery that we were cousins.

Bonding in this fashion allowed both of us to become acquainted with each other's families. So the more I got to know Melvin, the more I got to know his family. Especially, I became better acquainted with his father who was known only as "Mr. Franklin."

Now Mr. Franklin was always cool with me. But you know how that "when we get behind closed doors" saying goes.

According to Melvin, Mr. Franklin was that dad from that place called the "bottomless pit." Straight outta Willie Wonka's chocolate factory, Mr. Franklin wasn't coming home to dinner with mints to put on your pillow. Again, the gospel according to Melvin, there was nothing sweet about Mr. Franklin figuratively or literally.

But I will say, in Melvin's defense, Melvin was my friend. And I was going to be down with my friend through the thick and the thin.

With regard to Mr. Franklin's offense, I didn't see Frankenstein, Dr. Jekyll, or Mr. Hyde. Mr. Franklin impressed me as a quiet and peaceful kind of guy. But what could I know, being on the outside looking in? The only thing I could see was Melvin's low self-esteem. And I didn't have to be Sigmund Freud to see that.

At my young age, I was totally confused. I could not decide whose situation was the worst—Melvin's or mine. To have a father living outside of the home was bad. But to have one living inside the home who was continually being pointed to as the source of all your mental anguish had to make you wanna holla. So I just threw up both my hands.

When you are a kid, you see things "with a child's heart," just like Stevie said. Melvin's childish heart saw his father differently than I was able to see from my vantage point. But with my "childish heart," Melvin was my friend. Being my friend from a child's perspective colored me loyal. If Melvin said his old man was this, that, and the other, I wasn't knowledgably equipped to say otherwise. So out of respect for my not-so-distant cousin and the Franklin family, my name was Ness, and I tried my best to stay out of any mess. God knows I had my own to deal with as previously said.

During my wonder years, my mom worked very hard to teach Robert and me to be respectable. By respecting others, we learned to respect ourselves. Through self-respect, we gained a large measure of self-confidence. It was self-respect and self-confidence that boosted my brother's self-esteem and mine. In the matter of Melvin, such was not the case. With regard to my best friend, I was his sole supporting cast.

But why am I telling you all of this about my best friend? My brother from another mother? Where am I headed? How about all the way to Emerald City? Right down the yellow brick road!

Did you ever give some serious thought to why that scarecrow, tin man, and lion were really off to see the wizard? Well, you know it can be summed up in two words. Low self-esteem!

Those three characters allowed somebody to run a serious mind game on them. The scarecrow bought into the belief that he didn't have a brain. The tin man accepted the proposition that he didn't have a heart. The lion embraced the notion that he was a coward.

Just how do you think the scarecrow, tin man, and lion arrived at those self-debilitating thoughts in the first place? Dorothy didn't tell them that they were screwed up in the mind, body, and soul respectively. She found them that way! That means whomever they were hanging with prior to Dorothy did a number on their individual heads.

Did the scarecrow have a papa who continually called him a stupid son of a pitch?

Did the tin man have a Tin-Lizzy? A wife who was always on his case?

Was it the lion's mama who got him thinking he was gay? Did she treat him like he was a dandelion?

The only thing those three got from the Wiz was a realization they had nothing to get in the first place. What each wanted or thought they needed, they already possessed from the start. So here and now, how many are still psychologically off to see the wizard? Just how many folks are following those yellow bricks to an Emerald City that offers nothing but dead-end streets with mirrored walls?

When I met Melvin Franklin, he was the scarecrow, tin man, and lion all rolled up into one. A blunt ready to be smoked then flicked to the curb.

Melvin not only felt he was stupid, ugly, and ill equipped to face his own shadow, but he also despised his remarkable voice! Now, just how does an eight-year-old kid arrive at such psychologically depreciating conclusions? An eight-year-old boy just doesn't wake up one day and say, "I hate myself," without some kind of outside-of-his-own-head help.

One of the greatest, most popular and most recognizable voices in recorded history once belonged to a kid who wanted to throw it all away! A kid who knew not what he had! A kid who knew not because no one other than another kid was willing to tell him! Out of the mouth of a babe, being myself, Melvin was hipped to the value of his own magnificent voice.

As Melvin's best friend, I constantly told him not to be embarrassed about the fact that his voice was deeper than the voices of all others in our school and on our block. I told him that he should be proud of that fact. There was no reason to be ashamed! But I remember Melvin would say, "But folks laugh at me. They tell me I sound funny!"

I'd counter by saying, "Melvin, one day that voice of yours is going to make you real popular. It's going to make you famous!" You see, when you're eight going on something much more than nine, you know "what's happening." I knew what was happening! I knew my best buddy had skills.

Yet and still, if a toxic environment surrounds an individual, it's hard to receive a breath of fresh air. (Even when it's being blown directly into your face!)

But who was I to be telling someone that's only seven days my junior that everything is cool with the way he sounds? I didn't wear a skirt, so there wasn't going to be any "love connection" jumping off my opinion. I wasn't the toughest kid on the block, so there wasn't going to be any promotions made in my army, crew, or posse. Even though Melvin and I were ace spoons, partners to the end, thick and thin, and all that jazz, he didn't give doodley-squat about what I thought concerning that voice of his.

Remember Froggy on the *The Little Rascals*? If you don't, Google him. Well, Mel could go a fathom or two deeper. As a matter of fact, there were boyz in our hood who would call Melvin "Froggy." That saying about how cruel kids can be was coined on my street.

Needless to say, Froggy was a name Melvin hated. But when considering that a little white dude with a froggy-sounding voice wasn't much of a role model for a little black dude living in Detroit, it didn't take a student of Freud's to figure this thing out. So to eliminate the negative, we accentuated the positive by giving Melvin another handle: a cool nickname to go with that deep voice.

My mother kept hearing a song over and over on the radio called "Mel-Blue." She told Melvin that she was going to start calling him Mel-Blue.

Of course, Melvin thought the idea was great! And from that point on, instead of a "green with envy frog," Melvin became simply "Blue." What a difference a new name and a few days make! In time, Blue became more and more confident in himself.

Now, Blue's daddy, Mr. Franklin, wasn't a rolling stone. He didn't go nowhere. And he wasn't no ways tired of being an Al Bundy with doubled-up fists. As a matter of fact, kicking Buck's ass (the Bundy dog) became just an evening appetizer. But then and again, that was the gospel truth according to Melvin.

As a matter of unsubstantiated fact, the only reason I even bring the Franklin family matters up is because it illustrates my triumph over tribulation point. Making love, not war, can also make babies into men despite age or mind-set.

But again, whether true or false as it pertains to Mr. Franklin's relationship with his son, in Melvin's mind, Mr. Franklin was a thorn in Melvin's side. Both he and I had to deal with it.

Try to imagine the challenges associated with becoming who Melvin became as an adult with a thorn in his side as a kid? Whether fact or fiction, "as a man thinketh," the good book says, "so is he."

Since Melvin thought his dad was a tyrant that was a cross Melvin had to bear on his own, I was neither old enough nor strong enough to be a Simon from Cyrene. But being Melvin's friend meant I couldn't be Simple Simon either.

Melvin's cross was not and could not be mine to carry. I could only be there to listen to him groan and moan without passion or prejudice.

According to Melvin, things got so bad in the Franklin household that a plot was devised to put Mr. Franklin out of his family's misery!

Melvin, all by himself, came up with a serious plan to kill his ole man! The only thing that stopped him from carrying out his plot was a golden opportunity.

Since eight-year-olds back in my day didn't have guns, they couldn't do a "drive by." So what Melvin planned was a "drive over." Melvin would hide in the family car and wait for a clear shot. Fortunately, for both Melvin and his dad, Mr. Franklin never positioned himself directly in front of their automobile!

Well, I take that back. He did once. But it happened to be one of those Detroit winters where the streets had iced up. So when Mr. Franklin was target center with Melvin behind the wheel, the tires could only spin in one spot when the pedal hit the medal.

What if Melvin had been capable of rolling like those Menendez brothers? They are the two dudes who took out both their parents. And, in case you've forgotten, the "take out" I'm talking about ain't referring to dinner and a movie.

Yes, Virginia, there is a God in heaven who watches over the just, as well as the so-called unjust, the good as well as the so-called bad and the ugly. So even though this little boy Blue lived in a household that was filled with anger and confusion, I personally discovered the transforming power of true friendship. How a handshake, a pat on the back, a kind word spoken can get rid of more crap than a shovel.

That doesn't mean the crap won't boomerang. It only means the pile is prevented from getting too high—all at one time.

In our time of life, Melvin and I went through a whole lot of shovels. Those were our wonder years. Looking back on them when we were both with the Tempts, we would often wonder how we ever made it as far as we did. Of course, those were the years before such singularly recognizable names as Smokey, Elvis, Marvin, Diana, Michael, and the like.

Those were the days of Frankie Lymon and the Teenagers, Little Anthony and the Imperials, the Coasters, the Platters.

Those were the days when a 1957 Chevy was the bomb! Not because it was a classic, but because it was a brand-new ride. Straight off the assembly line right there in our own backyard. That place called Detroit, Michigan—the Motor City.

I sometimes think how different life would have been if I hadn't had that extended family who stood watch over me. Those were my guardian angels.

If my mama had not been the mother she was. If there had been no one there to give a damn about me but me. What if I had had to manage myself with my own childish heart?

In scientific terms, I sometimes think something termed the domino effect would have been dramatically called into play. What if I had been an eight-year old knucklehead? Would my knuckleheaded influence have impacted my best friend Melvin?

In addition to the domino, there would have been a butterfly effect. If I had supported Melvin in his effort to "chill" his father, both Melvin and I would have gone straight to jail. The Temptations we know today would have never been. And if the Temptations we know today had never been, then you would not be doing what you're doing now (reading this book).

Now, if you're not reading this book, what else would have changed in your life by the mere fact that whatever led up to you getting this book never would have physically happened! Cause and effect brings about consequences and repercussions that interrupt the time space continuum. (I picked that up watching the History Channel. When you're on the road held up in a hotel room, you watch a whole lot of cable TV!)

If I had been raised to entertain unbridled passion and prejudice, spinning tires would not have been the end of it. Just as there are Detroit winters, there are also Detroit summers. Martha Reeves and the Vandellas knew sooner or later that there would be a heat wave.

Just because ice melts to water when it gets hot, if I had had a mother other than the one I had, I may have been the one encouraging Melvin to wait until the winter ice melts on the street, instead of in his heart.

How different life would have been if Melvin had run over his dad, and I would have aided and abetted.

How many young guys and gals are incarcerated today for succeeding in doing what Melvin failed to do, because I had failed to encourage righteousness?

How could we have prepared for success as Temptations if we had fallen prey to temptations of a selfish act? An act having premeditated criminal intent!

Yes, back there in that day, that deep, powerful voice of Melvin Franklin's was just a "still, small one," crying in the wilderness. It was a voice not even trying to be heard.

But by the grace of God, Melvin's (and mine) was a voice that one day became heard, not only on the street where we both lived but also all around this big, wide "ball of confusion" world.

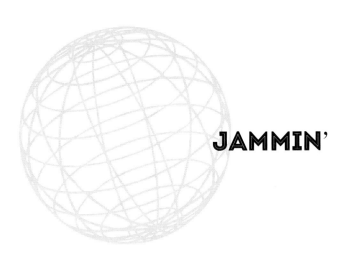

JAMMIN'

Shoe shines were a dime, and a penny could buy you plenty.

I was actually the Fonz, but everybody called me Richie. Yeah, these were the sho'nuff for real happy days!

Not only "shoe-shoe" shines, there were ten-cent pop machines too. That's right, soda pop in a glass bottle. We had a choice other than Pepsi and Coca-Cola in a can.

There was red pop, orange pop, green pop, blue pop. Back in them there days we even had yellow pop. The Dells could sing a rainbow; we could drink ourselves one too!

As a matter of fact, for a nickel you could even "double your pleasure and double your fun" with some chewing gum. And anything that had *hostess* written on it costs twelve cents— including tax!

A three-bedroom house was about ten grand. The average annual income was about $5,000 and some change. And it seemed like a "gulf" war was raging somewhere every other week. That's "gulf" as in gas!

I mean twenty-seven cents a gallon over here! A quarter a gallon over there! Nineteen cents a gallon around the corner! Or how about just a plain o' free fill up to go with that $1,700 new Ford that just rolled off the assembly line!

Yes siree. Life was good for a junior high school kid during the mid-1950s in Detroit, Michigan. After all, the Motor City was a world away from Selma, Birmingham, Montgomery, and the like.

Of course, in those days we didn't have us any MJs. (That's Michael Jordans and Magic Johnsons.) Our role models were found in names like Joe Louis and Jackie Robinson. Back then leather gloves were a fashion statement. Joe wore leather around his fists. Jackie had leather wrapped around his left hand. These were the dudes us preteens wanted to be like. But the more things change, the more some things remain the same.

Smokey cut a 1960s-something tune entitled "Can You Love a Poor Boy?" Strangely, it became a 1950s national anthem. In other words, what kind of loving can a poor boy get if he don't play sports? In other words, if you couldn't be something like Joe or Jackie, either a General MacArthur or a General Motors had the answer to all of your financial woes.

Now if you don't know who I'm referring to by General Mac, when I was singing with the Monitors, we had a hit called "Greetings (This Is Uncle Sam)." General Mac will forever be one of Uncle Sam's favorite nephews. And if you didn't have a silver spoon in your mouth, you were a prime candidate to be given a brass one engraved "US Army." So a very realistic expectation for any kid growing up on my block was either an automobile assembly line or a military service induction line.

Bottom line, if you were a kid on my block, your only backstage pass to fame and fortune was very limited. If you didn't have Joe or Jackie skills, you best be able to make up the deficit with some way better than average musical dexterity.

Every morning I get up, I thank God I was blessed to get down! God Almighty, not only blessed me but also all of my run-around pals with the musical dexterity to not only "take it to the bridge," as James Brown would tell Maceo, but to take it on over. And one of those kids who could take it way beyond over was a twelve-year-old girl by the name of Norma Tony.

I used to go over to Norma's house every other day and listen to her play the piano. She played better than anyone I had ever heard. Watching her play was like magic. Her fingers seemed to softly glide over each key, making every note beautiful. I was so mesmerized by Norma that I decided to learn how to play. And, with her as my teacher, learn I did!

After school, when anyone asked, "Where are you going, Rich?" I'd enthusiastically holler, "Practice!" as I'd take off running down the street. The field of dreams, however, was that trove of 88 ebonies and ivories.

Now, I found myself going over to Norma's every day to practice on her piano. And as time went by, I began playing pretty good. So good, that I felt my performance needed to become a shared experience. And since I was never short on courage, I went looking for an audience.

Since nobody I knew other than Norma had a piano, I took my talents, without formal invitation, to a Senior Citizen's home. Like a warrior looking for a battlefield, I was an entertainer looking for a stage.

I played that old folks' home piano until my fingers felt numb. And the bedridden, sick, and elderly enjoyed my playing as much as I did. Even though I only knew one song!

Yes, "Your Precious Love" by Jerry Butler and the Impressions, in the key of C.

That's right, "the ice man cometh" in the twelve-year-old form of me. And my audience loved it! They made me feel like I was that dude in the movie *Casablanca*. Every time I would finish, somebody in the audience would yell, "Play it again...Sam!" And that's exactly what I did. I played it again, and again, and again, and again, and again.

So as more and more time went by, I began playing even mo' better. My skills began to draw an even larger audience. The activity room was packed. The joint was jumpin'. And now I'm even taking requests! I mean here I am in the old folks home at age twelve, and we be jammin'.

Yes, playing that "house" is where my ear and my vocal skills were perfected. Playing that house is where my courage and confidence as a public performer was first and foremost forged. I had me my very own "club." A place where I was the headliner! The star! The marquee name written in red crayon was mine! I was playing a house that nobody else wanted, and I was loving it. But, most importantly, my audience was loving me.

Yes siree, God had the hook-up, and he gave it to me. But I was having too much of a James Brown "good God" thing to be keeping all the fun to myself. It was just too much for a twelve-year-old kid to handle alone.

When the classic "Why Do Fools Fall in Love?" by Frankie Lymon and the Teenagers first hit, I desperately tried to mimic the bass. But my voice just couldn't go that low. All of a sudden Melvin came to mind. With me singing Frankie's alto, I knew Blue could match up perfectly with the background bass.

Needless to say, we began to practice and practice and practice and practice!

Being musically inclined made learning my varying parts real easy. When it came to Melvin, however, it was a totally different story. Blue was not anywhere near being musically anything.

Melvin's adolescent artistry was analogous to a Mack Truck engine being held up inside of a Volkswagen body! And given the fact that I was neither a certified mechanic nor bass singer, my job of teaching Melvin the correct notes was very difficult to virtually impossible. As we rehearsed, I found my voice tiring out because I had to constantly attempt to sing the correct bass notes.

The more I tried reaching deep down low for the notes that Melvin was supposed to sing, the more my voice began fading. Nevertheless, we were determined to get it right no matter how hard or how long it took. And eventually, my voice did do a disappearing act. And I developed a seriously sore throat.

A fringe benefit, however, from playing the old folks' home was the fact that old folks know old remedies for whatever it is that ails you. I'm talking about stuff you don't have to go to a pharmacy to get. Stuff that's right there in your kitchen cabinet or growing somewhere in somebody's backyard!

My sore throat was gone faster than a welfare check. Melvin and I were back on the case with renewed vim and vigor. I was determined he was going to learn how to manage that Mack Truck voice of his. Melvin was determined to let me steer him in the right direction. And we were persistent!

By being persistent, persistence met us at the piggy bank. We not only mastered that Frankie Lymon tune, but we also threw down on a whole bunch of others. Blue was doing that bass thing of his like he'd been doing it since he was the fruit of the womb.

Finally, we had us a door-to-door duet. And in them days, if you were twelve and had it going on, door-to-door do-wopping was cute to the tune of at least twenty dollars a day! And, with inflation the way it wasn't, twenty bucks divided by two could buy a whole lot of bubble gum.

But as is the case with any such business endeavor, growth and experience means expansion. A neighborhood friend known as Maceo Williams joined our twosome. And with a name like Maceo, you know he had to be good! So all of us would park on Melvin's front porch practicing our harmonic vibe.

Then our threesome added two more: Barbara Martin and Theodore Martin. We were now the fabulous five. When my idols Frankie Lymon and the Teenagers made their exit, we were ready to fill the gap center stage. We called ourselves the Imperials until we discovered that a dude known by the name Little Anthony had beaten us to the punch. But we didn't even care because we were good and nobody could tell us diff!

Now, if you're thinking it's all beginning to sound like a big ego trip, you're wrong. In those days, it wasn't about ego. It was strictly about the affirmation of self. It was about having a bold kind of confidence that would get you off the wall to ask the girl of your dreams for a dance. Even if you knew you were wearing mismatched socks with two left shoes, it was feeling good about who you are despite what you weren't.

I mean if you hadn't developed a positive sense of self by the time you'd reached your teens, the chances of you being a showstopper were probably about as good as that hell-bent snowball's.

For example, take a television show like *Star Search* or *Showtime* at the Apollo. Ask yourself what kind of personality is required to do your thing in front of such an audience. Even if you are the singer you think you are? Even if you are the dancer you think you are? Even if you are the comedian you think you are? It takes more thought than a mere "I think I can."

A half-stepping or semi–self-defeatist attitude is not the breakfast of champions. If you've got the slightest notion you'll drown in the ocean, you best stay out of the water and on the safety of the shore. You might as well keep singing in the choir or playing the neighborhood bar and grill.

To be a public performance entertainer that's worth more than the price of admission, you have to believe you are something special. You have to believe that you are one of the best at whatever it is you do. What the public thinks is always the final say. But those first thoughts always begin with you. And that's what both literally and figuratively sets the stage for success.

Unquestionably, there is a psychology for success that goes way beyond raw talent. A whole bunch of folks I've encountered along the way have talent. But they've never seen the bright lights and the big city from a chauffeur-driven limousine. Star quality minus star attitude never equals stardom. A body that's missing the heart and head for success is also missing the soul. And raw talent without soul is a terrible thing to waste.

So any player who's really got game always comes ready to play. If you don't have a "get ready, 'cause here I come" attitude, it's probably because you ain't!

You see, there's a certain mentality that all performing artists must have that transcends remarkable ability. It's bigger than ego, and it's deeper than Psych 101. What it is, is a simple "know." The simple ability to know that you're *badd*, as in better than just being good.

Not many groups had the sounds of Melvin's deep bass coupled with the smooth alto of Maceo, Barbara, Theodore, and me. And, the trip part, we hadn't even entered high school! Back to that popular expression of the day, Eliot Ness and his boyz had nothing on us. As far as we were concerned, we were the Untouchables.

And we knew it! But to be a Temptation one day, we had to know it way before we could show it. Certainly, we had to know something other than our name and address.

The "jammin" I was doing then established the confidence required to do it later on a much bigger stage.

Could the jammin' of the Motown era be realized today?"

Probably not.

Why?

Today's era is about individualism. The group concept is not "your American idol." Neither is it "the voice."

Yes, Diana became the prefix for the Supremes; Martha, for the Vandellas; Smokey, for the Miracles. But it was still the group concept from whence those individuals evolved. Today individualism begets individualism. A modern-day singer evolving from a group is as foreign to modern American music as an eight-track cassette is to playing modern American music.

Regardless of where we as individual Temptations ended up careerwise, because we individually started our careers singing in a group, the foundation was laid psychologically establishing our group as being bigger than the sum total of its individual five parts. The reason the Temptations in name survives today illustrates the fact that the Temptations' name or brand is bigger than any one of its members.

Otis Williams never sang lead on any of the Temptations' major hits. As a matter of fact, Otis never sang lead on any of the Temptations' minor hits, yet he tours the country at the writing of this book with four other individuals calling themselves Temptations who were not even alive when each of the songs they are now singing hit the charts.

I had the honor, privilege, and pleasure of contributing to a Temptations' hit with my voice as the lead singer. Of course, so did David Ruffin, Eddie Kendricks, Paul Williams, Melvin Franklin, Dennis Edwards, Damon Harris, and Ali Woodson.

The Temptations as a singing group today survives on the memory of "the way we were" and has very little, if anything at all to do, with the way they (the so-called Temptations) now currently are with Otis.

This is not meant to be disparaging as far as Otis Williams is concerned. It's just a statement of fact that the Temptations as individuals were about the business of being a singing group first, before becoming solo artists second. Let's put the real in it and keep it there. Those who pay to see the Temptations sing today and tomorrow are "driftin' on a memory" in much the manner of what my man Ronald Isley is crooning in "For the Love of You."

It is for the love of those twenty-something Temptations' top ten singles and thirty-something top ten albums that hit the pop charts during the 1960s through 1980s that drive audiences to see the Temptations today. Hearing "My Girl" sung today by Otis and company reminds you of "Your Girl" sung by David, Eddie, Paul, Melvin, and Otis way back when it was first released.

When those dudes from Australia sing "You Really Got a Hold on Me," does their singing really have a hold on you?

The answer, of course, is the fact that if it hadn't been for some dudes by the name of Ronnie White, Pete Moore, Bobby Rogers, and William Robinson, along with a lady by the name of Claudette Robinson, there wouldn't have been anything for those Aussie boys to really hold on to now!

Don't get it twisted. See and hear "the way we do the things we do" now for what they really are. The music lives today because of what it was.

Back in the day, it was all about the singing group first and foremost. Without the "back in the day" group mentality as the formation foundation, Motown would have been a morass—with emphasis on the last half of that word.

When a solo career became the overriding priority at Motown, that's when Master Gordy had to do some kung fu fighting and say, "Grasshopper time to leave."

As Temptations, it was our individual skill sets that collectively enabled the group to become what it became and remains today in name only.

Today, however, a different game is played. In this day and age, the Motown era cannot be duplicated because today's culture cultivates and promotes individuality. And strictly because of the individuality mentality, you have *American Idol*, as opposed to "American Idols"; *The Voice*, instead "The Voices"; and the concept of duets, which promotes one amateur paired with one celebrity.

Melvin and I began to see the big picture before it took form. It materialized only because we both worked hard to lay the foundation for future success while it basically resided as a figment of our preteen imaginations. The big picture for us was "the group." The group was bigger than that one solitary individual.

The way we did the things we were able to do as Temptations was the "soul" result of our "getting ready" at a very early age. Playing that old folks' home prepared us for the big break that we knew would one day come.

Indeed, of a truth, we were "jammin' until the break of dawn."

A LOVE SUPREME

If seventh grade was a bomb, junior high school was the blast. Here I was. A teenager. I was an oyster, and the world was my pearl. Being a junior high school student opened all kinds of doors for me. Or maybe being older and street-smarter allowed me to open all kinds of doors for myself.

As I watched my boyish body mature, my interests turned to pursuits other than just singing. I suddenly discovered I was just as gifted athletically as I was musically.

You see, junior high expands your universe. It propels you outside of the solar system you've grown accustom to seeing. I mean, what if you woke up one morning and saw two suns in the sky? Or you went out at night and saw a full moon in the east and a half moon in the west? You just might say, "Damn. Let me check this out!"

Well, that's just what I said, "Damn. Let me check this out!"

Being in junior high, I found out that I could really play me some baseball. Throw me either a fastball or a curve, and it was going, going, gone!

Being in junior high, I found out that I could really play me some football. Send me deep and you was beat!

Being in junior high, I found out that I could really play me some basketball. Eighty-five percent from the line! Seventy-five from the field!

And being in junior high, I also found out that hommie could play himself some hockey! That's right. I could skate. Backward as good as forward! And I could puck it as good as any my age had pucked it before. Seriously, you would have thunk Bobby Hull or the Great One had been my personal coach!

Yes, in junior high, there was a lot more to see besides the sun, moon, and planets I had been used to orbiting. My space shuttle, in the form of a big, ugly, yellow school bus, had finally allowed me to boldly go where my young, thought-I-knew-it-all behind had never gone before. And when I said, "Come in Houston, the eagle has landed," it was one small step for me and one giant leap for my mannish mind.

Yes, I was at the sho'nuff for real Cooley High—junior-high style. But the music heard in the movie wasn't spinning on any record player here. "Ooo Baby Baby" was an inspired thought just waiting to be penciled. And the inspiration necessary to prompt the penciling was all around. I'm talking about girls! Girls! Girls!

Just like I said, "I watched my boyish body mature, and my interests turned to pursuits other than balls, bats, and hockey pucks."

I remember the first time I saw her. She was very popular—even then. Her legs were long and skinny, and her hair was very short. And "them there eyes"!

She was my kind of girl. She was my "starship." That one my man Michael Henderson sings about!

Anyway, from the first day I looked into "them there eyes," and she looked into mine, we saw all the way into each other's souls. We became the best of friends—soul mates.

There is always something special about your first time love that you never forget. I think it's that certain innocence. That certain nonexpectation. That certain stupidity that makes you laugh decades later if time has allowed you to grow any wiser.

My starship and I didn't think about what-ifs. What if this, what if that. We didn't have a care in the world other than each other.

Now, being the man I knew I was, discovering this softer, gentler side of self was just like a car slamming on the brakes at a cruising speed of a hundred miles per hour. I mean, the football helmet I wore was XXL. Not to mention, with my last name being Street! Well, you best believe nobody could tell this little Richard anything. My "street" knowledge was my ticket to ride farther than any yellow bus could ever take me.

So here I was singing me a Billy Ocean tune that had yet to be written: "Suddenly," I was sho'nuff in love. I fell awake once I unexpectedly, without warning, looked into them there eyes.

My starship had changed my life. Her very soft and tender ways taught me what it was like to be in love with someone. You know, there is a big difference between loving someone and being *in love* with someone. Since we've all been there, I don't need to elaborate on those differences.

Anyway, my first love taught me how to really care! And her tender caring eventually showed me the difference between fairy tale infatuations and "I'll wash your dirty drawers with hand soap."

With all these lessons in store, I immediately knew she was definitely the fourteen-year-old "woman" for me. The girl of my dreams. And this feeling was mutual. If the two songs had been written, I would have been singing, "I got sunshine on a cloudy day." And she would have been echoing Mary Wells: "I'm sticking to my guy like a stamp to a letter."

As a matter of fact, Mary Wells, who made "My Guy" a hit, attended our school!

Now, interestingly enough, my starship could also sing. So you know we could really relate. And she had two girlfriends who sang with her. And at that time, their claim to fame was a song made famous by Ray Charles called "The Nighttime Is the Right Time."

When these three girls sang this song, my love would loudly hit the high notes that said, "Baby!" And when she did that, the various crowds would go crazy. This trio of girls sounded so good it inspired me to start a singing group with them, which also included my partner Melvin.

Needless to say, after telling Blue about the idea of forming a group with the girls, he was ecstatic. And since the girls all lived close to my starship, the practices were usually held at her house.

Almost every day Melvin and I would catch the city bus and transfer three times one way just to get to her house. On the days we missed the bus or couldn't afford to catch it, we'd walk.

The distance seemed like it was at least twenty miles.

So on those walking days, instead of Billy Ocean, we'd be singing us some yet-to-be-written Edwin Star: "Twenty-five miles from home and my feet are getting mighty tired!"

Perhaps you're beginning to see the inspiration behind all of those great Motown hits! We lived, at a very young age, all of the stuff those song lyrics talked about.

Yes, we were fourteen going on forty-five. And, the *forty-five* being referred to here is those plastic record discs we'd soon be making that would capture everything "going on" in our young hearts as adolescents.

Again, the Smokey Robinsons, the Holland-Dozier-Hollands, and the Norman Whitfields didn't just pull their material out of a hat. They pulled it out of life!

Now, "my girl" lived in a set of projects that were identical to all of the other projects in the area. In the beginning, finding her house was like finding a needle in a haystack. But once Melvin and I made it to her place, she would call the other girls over to rehearse. They also lived in the same projects. They were also very nice, shy, and quiet.

Before rehearsals began, another young person would be called over to join us. He was a guitar player by the name of Marv Tarplin. Marv later became Smokey Robinson's right-hand man and a successful songwriter.

The "do-do-do-do, do-do-do-do-do-do-do, do-do-do-do, do-do-do-do" on the front end of Smokey's "Tracks of My Tears" is Marv Tarplin doing his thing.

Remember such Marvin Gaye tunes as "Ain't That Peculiar"? "I'll Be Doggone"? "Take This Heart of Mine"? "One More Heartache"? Well, that's Marv Tarplin doing his thing!

Again, keep in mind the foundation for all of those hits that are still being sung and even sampled today was being laid when we were only in junior high! Yes, today's artists, who basically lack the creative talent we had as mere kids, may legally get away with blurring the lines between copyright infringement and outright stealing, but everyone who isn't tune deaf knows a Motown sound from a "Fly, Robin, Fly" thick-as-thieves imitation.

God blessed us with a gift, and we had to use it. For sure, it was nothing, but God that made that happen.

By no means am I a prophet, but please indulge me while I prophesize. Five will get you ten that forty years from now, the music that is predominantly popular in the black community today will not be sung or rapped as fluently as the tunes we dropped on the world.

I fully understand that folks don't like comparing eras of art. Could Muhammad have put a whuppin' on Mike? Could Joe Frazier have put a whuppin' on Mike? (Could Mike have put a whuppin' on Mike!)

Be all of that as it may, the music we made back in the day was simply a special occasion. I'll say without hesitation that it will never be duplicated or happen like that again. The creative Spirit of God touched everybody remotely connected with the Motown era. And by *remote*, I'm talking about all who lived during the time who either bought a record or just snapped their fingers to the beat.

You see, the Motown fans were just as significant as the Motown artists. If the creative Spirit of God had not touched the masses of people to the tune of buying those tunes, Motown would have been Ghostown.

The Motown era included both artists and fans. That's why on all of those early albums, they are written with "The Sound of Young America!"

The Motown era is a generation. Just as Genesis says, "The Spirit of God moved upon the face of the waters," only the Spirit of God can move upon the faces of people to impress them to buy millions and millions and millions of records. Now I'm talking about millions and millions and millions of records from a black company that was jump-started in a small residential house on the east side of Detroit.

Now, that's a miracle that has nothing to do with Smokey's!

Getting back to my girl, altogether, we'd get together and practice our harmonics. I will never forget the great ketchup sandwiches we'd have for a snack. Since all of our families were struggling, having ketchup on the bread was often considered a delicacy! Sometimes, depending on whose house we were at, the sandwich spread was just sprinkled sugar!

And as far as a beverage? Well, 90 percent of the time it was sugar water. We couldn't even afford the luxury of Kool-Aid!

But because God is good even when you don't realize he's there, we didn't mind the hardships. Our music was our nourishment. It gave us a spiritual connection that was food to both our individual and collective souls.

Truly, this soul food God has given has been my "bread of life" for a lifetime!

Anyway, my starship sang background during this time. She had a voice that was a very high-pitched first soprano. When she sang, everyone listened!

One of the other girls had a medium alto-pitched sound while the other, also an alto, had a voice that was more powerfully pitched.

It was this girl's stronger voice that normally landed her the majority of the group's leads. Altogether, the three voices blended perfectly.

For us guys, I had perfected a multiranged voice. It was versatile enough to allow me to sing anywhere I was needed. Melvin's voice was now even deeper. Nobody in town could even come close to copying his sound. Marv didn't sing; he just let his fingers do the walking.

Starting with my girl's high soprano, all the way down to Melvin's gutbucket bass, we were something to behold. Our group sounded so good, the long bus rides were just a minor inconvenience. Besides, we were just a group of teenagers who enjoyed doing what we did best from age fourteen to fifteen.

And, of course, it also didn't hurt that one of the girls and I were sweethearts. Practicing just meant more togetherness.

In time, after many months of practicing, I began to take a closer look at my first love. I began to see there was something about her that was extra special. There was something that distinguished her from everybody else.

If you've ever watched somebody in the light of the moon before they've become as bright as the sun, you know exactly what I'm talking about. For example, take that person who walks into the room wearing clothes that look like they've been slept in. But without even hearing them utter a mumbling word, you just know there's more than what meets the eye.

This is the vibe my starship began to radiate. We were just kids, but we all knew there was something more than what was meeting either eye or ear. Unexplainably, there was a certain style and charisma.

There was also a look. That look you can't describe, but you know it when you see it. When you're fourteen years old and madly in love, everything is seen through rose-colored shades. And shades have a way of making everything look good.

So after nearly two years of practicing, the group became better and better. And so did the friendship that my starship and I shared. The gentle fire that had burned in our hearts had now raced south of the border. I mean, if you've ever had the pleasure of being in the tropics or some associated equatorial region, you know how hot it can get!

Remember Norma Tony from the previous chapter? Well, I went over to Norma's house to practice the piano. Once I got there, everyone had somewhere else to go. That left me all alone. The afternoon was cool and breezy.

As I sat there, all alone, I began thinking about my girl. I thought about how much I loved her. I also thought about making love to her and how we had talked about making love for months—almost a year. And I was now almost fifteen. Going on thirty!

As I thought to myself, I came up with a brainstorm. Norma's house is normally empty. It would be the perfect place to make love to my starship!

Because of all the family members at her house, making love there was not even considered an option. With my brainstorm in mind, I immediately made the call. "Hey, baby, this is me." After pausing, I smoothly said, "Remember when we talked about making love?"

"Yeah," she said.

"Well, why don't you meet me tomorrow. I have a place where we can go. A place where no one will bother us."

"Are you sure?" she said.

"Yes I'm sure. Can you come?"

"Oh, baby. Nothing can keep me from getting to you!" she said.

I remember I couldn't believe what I had heard! Especially after months of only talking about it. I just couldn't believe that we were actually going to go through with it. The only thing I could think about was the fact that tomorrow at this time I will be totally in the arms of the "woman" I love! The only thing left was to make sure everything was everything over at Norma's that forthcoming day.

And, of course, that meant everybody would be gone! There would be no unexpected changes in anybody's routine.

Nobody would get sick and have to stay home. The busses would be running. There would be no out-of-town visitors coming for some long extended stay.

You can't begin to imagine the assortments of what-ifs that began to mess with my mind. And the contingency plans I had come up with to keep from going crazy!

As the next day came, I prepared for my love's arrival. I was so nervous I didn't know what to do! I don't even think I slept one wink all that previous night. This was going to be my first time ever making love. And according to my love, it would be her first time too!

You see, this wasn't about sex. This was about love. I'm talking Peaches & Herb–type romance: "I love her and she love me. And, that's the way it's going to be." I mean, "we gonna be united!"

But I also knew I had to play it cool. There ain't no way I could let on that this was my first time too. I knew that I had to make her believe our sexual experience was going to be everything and more than she'd ever expected it to be. The only problem with that was the fact of me somehow assuring her that I actually knew what I was doing!

I mean, we was singers. We sang songs about love. We made love vicariously thousands of times through the spoken word. I was a 1950s Jason, and she was my "lyric." She was my "love," and I was her Jones. In other words, at the grand old age of almost-fifteen, we were both actually twice our age when you get right down to knowing the essence of all those ballads we had been singing.

I mean, "what if?"

"What if!"

I didn't even want to think about it. But it was still in the back of my mind.

Once she arrived, I couldn't believe my eyes. My wildest dreams were finally coming true. She looked so good that I couldn't take my eyes off her. And I felt her eyes passionately glued to me.

I lifted her off her feet and slowly took her downstairs to the basement where the piano was located. Once downstairs, we began passionately kissing. The more we kissed, the more the mercury in my thermometer began to rise.

As I slowly began taking her clothes off, she asked, "Are you sure you know what you're doing?"

"Sure, I'm sure," I said.

We continued kissing as I slowly continued to remove the rest of her clothes. All the way down to her toes. I could tell she was nervous to the point of being scared.

"Are you sure you know what you are doing?" she said.

"Sure, I'm sure," I repeated. After all, I had done this a thousand times in my head, I reassured myself.

But to gain her total confidence, and mine, I decided to explain the procedures that would take place in our close encounter of the first kind.

Interestingly, the more I attempted to convince her that everything was going to be okay, the more I convinced myself. Eventually, I gained her complete confidence as well as my own.

As all of my true love's clothes were now lying neatly folded on the floor, I thought to myself, *Where do I go from here? What do I do next?*

So, here was my starship. Here was my *Enterprise*. My two-year mission was just about to allow me to "boldly go where no man had gone before." The only problem: The course I had chartered was to a place where I had never gone before either.

As she looked straight into my eyes with her body nervously trembling, my body began to shake too. I took her into my arms and held her as tightly as I could. I gently laid her body back. It was just the two of us there in the basement—on a rather cold floor.

So, I began searching—and searching and searching. And the more I searched, the more I began to sweat. And sweat. And sweat. And sweat! I'm talking about a James Brown cold sweat.

The more I began to sweat, the more my sweat dripped and dripped and dripped on top of her smooth, silky body. Eventually we were both soaking wet. With all my sweat!

It was right then and there that I knew this young woman was very special. She realized that I was just as nervous and as scared as she happened to be—maybe even more. This was truly an embarrassing moment. This girl of my dreams could have done a number on my head that would have blown my manly sense of self totally away.

I mean here I was: a big perpetrator. And there she was: her first time. And I had ruined it for both of us. All kinds of stuff began to go racing through my mind. I was through, I knew. How could I ever face tomorrow when today was all I could see? My whole world ended!

But rather than destroying what little ego I had left, she was now cool, calm, and collected.

She said, "Baby, I'm here. I'm going nowhere."

And I guess it was hearing her say "baby" at that precise moment. Hearing her say it in the way that only she could say it touched me in a way I will always remember. Her words were poetry in motion inside of me. And that motion triggered an emotion that has managed to transcend space and time.

Well, it was at that precise moment in my life that I truly understood what a real woman's love and understanding really means.

And needless to say, it was also shortly after that precise moment that my "search" amazingly ended. I finally struck gold in more ways than one.

You see, more lasting than the sex, I now had a deeper and more enduring appreciation of the person, not just the young girl I loved.

Shortly after our lovemaking experience ended, my girl started going to another school. It was one of those circumstances beyond our mutual capabilities to prevent or control.

Even though we tried to deal with the situation and circumstance, things became just too difficult for us to see each other. The biggest problem was transportation.

And with regard to our singing group, Melvin and I lived way too far away to keep up with the late night and odd rehearsal schedules. So as a result of the long-distance separation, the romance I shared with my starship eventually crashed. And, of course, my heart was broken.

But God is good. Everything turned out all right for both of us. We had no idea that we'd ever be on something as big as *The Ed Sullivan Show*—or, bigger yet, that we would be traveling the whole wide world.

My starship was one of the shyest people I'd had ever met in my life. And, of course, she became one of the most famed singers and celebrities on the planet.

And, yes, most importantly, throughout the years, both of us have been able to smile, remember, and remain best of friends. She was the nicest person then, and "no wind, no rain, nor winter's cold can stop me" from being her friend till the end.

I guess my starship will always and forever be "my love supreme."

JOHN

Like earlier said, there is definitely a spiritual connection to the whole Motown thing. I guess that's why some chapters of my story are named the names that they are.

For example, take this chapter. "John" is a very significant name in the "greatest story ever told." And since this book is the greatest story I've ever told, the name "John" is very significant right here too!

How so? Permit me to explain.

At age fourteen, shortly after losing the love of my then life, I began working in a nightclub. This club was my first real gig. I played the piano to the tune of $100 per set. And I did at least two sets a week.

Now, because of my age, I wasn't supposed to come into contact with hard-liquor-drinking adults. But when you're viewed as having an exploitable talent, laws, rules, and regulations have a way of getting bent.

I didn't, however, mind the booze and R-rated behavior. The money I made enormously helped my mother with her financial responsibilities. Besides, I was doing something I loved to do. And getting paid for it!

Also, working in that nightclub taught me a whole lot about life as such pertained to women. Unlike my yesteryear, yesterlove, yesterday, there was now nothing on a female's body that I couldn't find in a Detroit second!

Actually, it is very interesting how sexual mores continue to go through changes. Today, if a fourteen-year-old boy gets caught up with a grown woman, the female typically gets time, and the boy gets counseling. Getting caught up back in my day means the only thing either gets is a reputation.

But older women who looked like anything back in my day just weren't interested in any fourteen-year-old kids. Despite how mannish we thought we were, there were just too many real men on the scene.

For a fourteen-year-old to blow a mature woman's mind, buddy boy had to have a serious repertoire and accessories to match—if you know what I mean.

So there was none of that "Hollywood summer of '42" stuff in the community where I grew. That's not to say buddy boy couldn't get lucky. I mean anyone could pick this week's winning lotto numbers if they tried real hard; and the moon, Venus, Mars, and Jupiter were in perfect alignment.

Suffice it to say, a kid on my street getting caught up with his teacher, somebody's mama, or an older woman was about as random as an Oscar-winning black actor or actress. That means our hands and hearts were filled with the girls who were either plus or minus one or two years our own age.

But, nevertheless, it was this interest in the opposite sex that put the pep in our step, the glide in our stride, and the soul in our stroll as we pursued opportunities that sometimes came sudden and unannounced.

Shortly after my high school entrance, a man named Billy Davis approached Melvin. Billy was part of a group called the Voice Masters, which later became the Originals.

The Voice Masters was in need of a bass singer, and the word around town was, "Melvin Franklin is the man."

Well, "the man" accepted the offer, and he was off to New York where he recorded his first record with the group. That record was entitled "Needed."

Needless to say, Melvin was so happy with the recording that he called me from New York to let me hear the song. I was very happy for him too. Neither of us could believe that he was actually singing on a real record. This experience was the start of something big for a one-time little boy who had lacked both self-esteem and confidence.

After this recording, Melvin met Otis Williams. Otis was the leader of a group called Otis Williams and the Distants. Otis had been looking for a bass singer for his group. He too was told that Melvin was the best man for the job.

Suddenly, Blue was faced with another proposition. Since he wasn't totally committed to the Voice Masters, teaming up with Otis wasn't that difficult a decision. And once another opening became available in the Distants, Melvin saw to it that I was brought on board.

Finally, Melvin and I were back in stride again! We were reunited. This time in a group that we really felt validated our musical existence and a future career.

Now the group was composed of Otis, Melvin, Eldridge Bryant (also known as Al), James Crawford (also known as Peewee), and myself.

Talk about practice? That's all we did! And during this time, I did most of the lead singing. All of us were focused and full of harmony.

As we rehearsed and perfected our sound, the word about us got around town. And this resulted in our meeting a woman by the name of Johnnie Mae Matthews.

Johnnie Mae worked for a record label that was based in Detroit called Northern Records. Through this label, Otis Williams and the Distants recorded its first two records, "Come On" and "Always."

During these studio sets, which were considered old-time sessions, we only had two microphones. One was for the lead singer and the other was for everybody else.

These microphones would be hooked up to a one-track or two-track tape recorder. That means everyone recording had to do their part and do it well, or else the entire recording session would have to be redone until the entire crew got it right. Time was the only margin for error. Subsequently, here is where I learned the true meaning of the expression "Time is money!" The more studio time it took to get it right, the more money it took to buy the studio time necessary to get it right!

As we recorded, we would gather outside the door of a little bathroom. Because of this bathroom's barren walls, our voices were amplified. Consequently, the reverberation of our harmonics inside this restroom made it our studio A.

After the success of "Come On" and "Always" and the novelty of hearing our voices on a radio had chilled, the business side of the business became more of a reality. Otis went to Johnnie Mae with a question concerning royalties. She told him, "Oh no! There's no royalties. There's nothing happening that big with your record."

To say we were shocked "hitless" is an understatement. We were hearing our record played on the radio every day. Sometimes four or five times a day! Can you imagine turning on a radio station in your city or a city the size of Detroit and hearing yourself on record a half dozen times a day for a solid month!

And then imagine being told you didn't have a hit.

Yes, we were shocked "hitless."

For us, that was a lot like Rodney King being told he really didn't get an ass whuppin' that night by the LAPD.

Now, I know my publisher would like me to be polite and say Rodney got his buttocks bruised. But in reality, an ass kicking is what Rodney got. When you get beat up by multiple billy clubs and kicked in your testicles, you are getting your ass kicked. There's just no polite way to literarily express that kind of situation.

I will, however, be polite in my literary expression of what Johnnie Mae Matthews was doing to us. We were getting screwed. I won't use that six-letter word that begins with the sixth-letter of the alphabet.

Being adults about everything other than that money thing, we were totally confused. But confusion is the last name in the main title of this book.

This experience with our very first label was only a sign of the things to come as far as polite literary expressionism. Being screwed by Johnnie Mae was merely a warning shot fired across our brow. We didn't, however, stay confused very long. The aromatic aroma of that "Taurus scatology" (*Taurus* is a polite name for *bull*; you should be able to figure the *scat* part without any help) disappeared very quickly!

The very next day, Johnnie Mae came into the record company wearing a brand-new everything. From hairdo to hair-don't, Johnnie Mae looked like she was about to be featured on the cover of next month's *Ebony*.

When asked about the sudden transformation, the only explanation given was she had just "hit the numbers!"

Of course, all of us in the group thought this was really some coincidence. Especially since we should have received some type of royalty check from our record at the same time she claimed to have hit that number.

Needless to say, Otis Williams and the Distants never saw a dime from our first recording experience. Nor did we ever become a big success with any future recordings under the auspices of Ms. Johnnie Mae Matthews. Our stay with Northern Records ended as abruptly as it had begun.

We thought this sistah was going to help us, and all she did was help herself. This is why it is important to surround yourself with people you know you can trust. If you don't or if you have to take someone at face value (like us), the odds are you will get (politely put) the short end of the stick.

Quite often celebrities are accused of having an attitude when it comes to dealing with the public in general and employees in particular. The only thing I can say is getting burned enough times around an oven instinctively causes carefulness when you open an oven door.

Back in the day there was a group by the name of Undisputed Truth. A big hit of theirs is entitled "Smiling Faces." Of course, they're talking about the kind of "smiley faces" that pretend to be your friend. And that "pat on the back that just might hold you back!"

In the course of two years, we had gone from the height of elation to the depth of despair. We were down. Way down. We desperately needed a miracle.

One day, completely out of the blue, we hear that Smokey Robinson has an in-town performance scheduled for Detroit's Family Theatre.

It was the early '60s, and Smokey was one of the hottest acts Motown had to offer. No other artist could match Smokey's smooth, silky high notes that seemed to make all the women melt. So Otis, Melvin, Al, Peewee, and I had to check the brotha out.

That night, into the concert theater, we walked cleaner than the Detroit Board of Health. We were on a mission with only two things in mind: (1) meet at least half of all of the women who were going to be in attendance and (2) see exactly how Smokey can do what he does. We knew that if we were ever going to be successful, we had to take notes from the then best.

Settled in our seats toward the back, Smokey was on stage all the way *live*. Instead of entertainers that night, the five of us were pupils with pen and pad.

"I will build you a castle with a tower so high, it reaches the moon. I'll gather melodies from birdies that fly and compose you a tune. Give you lovin' warm as mama's oven and if that don't do, then I'll try something new," Smokey sang.

And the women became girls gone wild! As a matter of fact, there were even some dudes off in the place that were acting a bit strange in reaction to Smokey's singing.

Anyhow, amid all the madness generated by Smoke's soul-stirring performance, we spotted Berry Gordy Jr. (the president and founder of Motown Records) going to the men's room.

All of a sudden, Otis gets this brainstorm that we should follow Berry into the men's room. Otis supposes that once we are all in there together, maybe we can meet Mr. Gordy and sing for him. Of course, we all thought that idea of his was ridiculous. Unquestionably, stupid.

But given the fact that we seemed to be in the slow lane to nowhere, the more we thought about Otis's idea, the less it sounded whack. We decided what the heck. After all, now was just as good a time as any to strut our stuff. We knew if we were ever going to make it big, here was our chance to seize the moment that could very well be our big opportunity.

So off to the "john" we went!

Once there, we came face-to-face with Mr. Motown—Mr. Berry Gordy Jr. himself.

With the name of our group being Otis Williams and the Distants, we unanimously decided that Otis would do all of the talking.

As Melvin, Peewee, Al, and I stood coolly in the background with smiles like a Cheshire cat's, Otis made the introductions and convinced Berry to give us a listen. And Berry, without seeming to give it a second thought, laughingly consented.

So right there in the men's room of Detroit's Family Theatre, we sang "Be Ever Wonderful" by Ted Taylor in a tightly rehearsed five-part a cappella harmony.

Yes, we threw down right there in the john!

Even though people were entering and exiting, even though water was running full force from iron as well as flesh faucets, even though toilets were sporadically and courteously flushing in an effort to filter the air, we were neither deterred nor distracted. We saw the brass ring and were determined to grab it.

Berry was very impressed with our sound. At least, that what he told us. He also said he would see us again. That he would get back to us later. That he would call. Obviously he spoke the truth.

Otis Williams, Melvin Franklin, and I went on to become members of the Temptations. Otis and Melvin, of course, were original members of the group. I wasn't so fortunate.

Why?

Well, that's the next chapter. But allow me to just say briefly in this chapter: In order for boys to be wise men, they absolutely have to be raised under the guiding influence of a man. Single mothers have and always will, by necessity, be essential to a son's growth process. But just as there are things that a mother can best get her daughter to understand, there are also things that only a father can best get his son to comprehend.

As street-smart as I thought I was, not having a dad impacted in ways I had no way of even beginning to sociologically and psychologically understand and comprehend until after graduating from the university of hard-knocks. Even though an extended family father figure might pick up the much-needed slack, there is no replacement for the in-house physical presence of a father-son relationship that's built on blind trust.

In case you haven't thought about it, blind trust doesn't come overnight, in a week, month, or year. It's developed from the cradle and hopefully lasts to the grave.

Just like a mother wants a relationship with her daughter that is based on "you can tell me anything," there's some stuff a son just isn't going to tell his mama. And if he did, there are some things that mama just wouldn't know how to effectively or sufficiently deal with in a manly manner.

God made the marriage of a man and woman for sociological and psychological reasons that have little, if anything, to do with politics.

Thinking like a man and acting like a woman is exactly what the world is today: a ball of confusion.

It's a game played for laughs until the she-and-he hawing is checked by the reality that there's more to a man-woman relationship than sex in ninety days or less. When a child's heart involuntarily becomes involved, that kid doesn't need his or her mother thinking like a man. And certainly that kid doesn't need his or her father acting like a woman.

Perhaps if my papa had been thinking like a real man and not acting like anyone or thing other, I would have been one of the original temptations—and not the guy literally and figuratively waiting in the wings. But that story is saved for another chapter too.

The important thing before closing the book on this chapter is the fact that Berry Gordy Jr. had a revelation that came by virtue of a john. It was a revelation that wound up being shared with the world—a world that tumultuously rests within its Creator's hands.

Even though at first we laughed at the idea of pursuing Berry into a restroom, we did it anyway. Instead of being timid and tentative, we knew what we wanted and had the spirit of confidence to go after it.

I believe God impressed Berry to see our spirit of confidence as well as our spirit of sincerity. Berry could have said hell to the no. He didn't have to give us the time of day or night.

How willing would you be to entertain the request of five teenagers who politely cornered you in a stank public restroom?

But admittedly, there was a certain less pretentiousness associated with the times back then. The artistic innocence of the era permitted us to bust a move on a 1960s Berry Gordy Jr. that may not be all good now.

Consider walking up to a twenty-first-century Berry Gordy counterpart whom you find in a john. Ask a simple question. Chances are you'll simply get checked before you get anywhere near your question's question mark?

You see, the early '60s was the threshold over which a political revolution was being ushered. Berry was receptive to us because us black Americans were becoming more receptive to ourselves.

Let's put the real in it. You cannot greet a man with, "What's happening, my brotha?" if you're intent on dealing with him like he's that "nigga in the alley," Curtis Mayfield sings about.

In that proverbial "process of time" that the Bible talks about, somewhere in between 1990 and now, "what's happening, my brotha?" has been replaced with, "C'mon, man." In case you didn't know, "Come on, man" is what you say when someone says or does something stupid.

Contemporaneously speaking, what we did in that john back in the day was stupid. It could have been a "C'mon, man" moment.

But because Berry didn't oversupport himself by being too important to receive our impromptu introduction, we were provided with a career-making opportunity that may have been a long time coming.

And because we as both individuals, and as a group, didn't undersupport ourselves by being too shy or artistically insecure to make an introduction, we didn't deny ourselves the career opportunity we were ultimately given.

I guess you can say "we weren't too proud to beg" Berry for a few minutes of his time. And I guess you can say he was neither too proud nor too big to give it.

I guess it also just goes to show that both "revelations" and "temptations" can sometimes be found in the exact same place.

DELILAH

Even though some temptations can be said to happen overnight, the Motown variety took a bit longer. If things "could of" or "would of" happened a bit faster, this chapter definitely "should of" been called something entirely different.

In the restroom of Detroit's Family Theatre, it was my voice that was included in the five-part harmony that auditioned for Berry Gordy Jr. And, as unquiet as it wasn't kept, it was my voice that was heard out front of the group. In other words, Richard Street was Otis Williams and the Distants' lead singer. It was Melvin's bass and my alto that gave Otis Williams and the Distants its "wow."

Now, I don't say that to discredit any of the other fellas. It just happens to be a fact. And if I'm going to put the real in it, I've got to tell it like it was.

It's not about any self-aggrandizement in a literary effort to say I was all that. The fact of the matter was we were all that way back in our long ago. And putting it mildly, I had a rather significant part to play. I wasn't just that "guy" standing in when one of the original Tempts was "high."

Whenever you watch that *The Temptations* TV show that was first aired on NBC back in 1998, you get the impression that I was a bench player. Using a basketball term, anyone viewing the show comes away with the notion that Richard Street was just a dude who would run in off the bench as the sixth man. Well, the truth be told; my contribution to the Temptations was a whole lot more than that there.

Now I realize when it comes to making movies and writing books, history often gets written as "his story" and not as what actually went down. Everybody knows the name of that game.

There are pyramids and statues over in Central and South America that look practically the same as the ones over in Africa that date back way before Christ. Yet Christopher Columbus gets the credit for discovering America in 1492.

Even though Christopher stopped off in West Africa way before he headed this way in order for the brothas to show him the way, "his story" is written in a manner that gives him all the credit.

Now, TV1 and/or BET ought to team up with the History Channel in order to do an "Unsung" on whomever that brotha or sistah was who told Chris which way to go. They need to find a Kunta Kinte look-a-like and show him telling Columbus to head out on a straight line that-a-way following that bright star to the bottom left of the bottom star in Orion's belt.

So I'm not going to slam Otis. I'm just gonna say, "C'mon, man!"

Fo' shizzle my nizzle (borrowing from my man Snoop), Otis did form the group called Otis Williams and the Distants. Yeah, if it hadn't been for Otis, there wouldn't have been any Otis Williams and the Distants. And, yeah again, if there hadn't been any Otis Williams and the Distants, there probably wouldn't have been any group staking its claim to fame as the Temptations. I'm more than willing to give credit and props where credit and props are due.

But, c'mon, man! If you are going to tell the story, keep it real by putting the real in it. You don't have to undersupport others to oversupport yourself!

If it hadn't been my voice out front that Berry Gordy heard in that restroom, would we as Otis Williams and the Distants gotten a Motown callback?

Do you think anybody auditioning front and center for *American Idol* gets a second chance to make a first impression?

Those of you who happen to be old-schoolers know full well that Harold Melvin and the Blue Notes did not find the ladies swooning over the vocal chords of their namesake Harold.

And with regard to the Gang, Kool may have been all that, but it certainly wasn't his singing that had folks celebrating!

The bottom line: Otis Williams was no lead singer. He wasn't in 1959, and throughout the lifespan of the Tempts, he's never been. I'm just not too timid or modest to say, Otis Williams and the Distants became Motown's Temptations because of what Berry Gordy heard in a Detroit john.

But still, be that as it may, my arms are still not long enough to pat myself on the back. And even though I'm six foot two, my legs are still too short to kick myself in the ass. Sometimes, it just is what it is.

The old folks are fond of saying, "God never gives you what you're not supposed to have."

Looking back over the years, I guess I shed some tears about that situation—me not being a member of the original Temptations. But in me finally becoming a member of the old folks' club, I now know and fully understand the magnitude and depth of that statement. God never gives you what you're not supposed to have because if he did, he would be taking that gift from the one who was supposed to have it. You can't give your son the same spot that your daughter is supposed to occupy.

When it comes to singing groups, coexistence beyond the self-imposed boundaries of individual limitations is nonexistent. Just as God Almighty wasn't willing to make a spot for an eleventh commandment, God Almighty wasn't feeling six-on-stage-at-the-same-time temptin' Temptations.

But the old folks are also fond of saying, "What goes around comes around."

I like to think just because Berry's first impression was swayed by the Richard Street and Melvin Franklin connection, there would somehow be another go round for yours truly. And just because 1 Corinthians 14:33 says, "God is not the author of confusion"; be it in the form of a ball or even a six-foot-plus square, there was another time and place for me.

Again, my saying this is not meant to diminish the role of Otis, Al, or Peewee. Once again, truth is just what it is. And one more time again, said as politely as I can say it, if it were not for Teddy Pendergrass, nobody other than Harold Melvin's family and friends would have known who in the heaven or hell Harold was as far as the Blue Notes.

And, likewise, if it were not for James (J. T.) Taylor, well, Robert "Kool" Bell's gang just wouldn't have rang as loud as they did.

What's in a name? Perhaps more than meets the eye or ear.

Otis Williams has always been "distant." Even though Otis's name was in the forefront, he was in body, mind, and soul a background vocalist. And Eddie Kendricks, David Ruffin, Paul Williams, Melvin Franklin, Dennis Edwards, Damon Harris, and Ali Woodson (all former Temptations lead singers) all agreed with me.

So in giving credit where credit is long overdue, even at the risk of tossing some of those Shakespearean "what's in a name roses" on a street where I lived, the Temptations' genesis is rooted in the obscury of my personal past.

The point being made, "if you make your own bed, you have to lie in it."

News quickly spread around Detroit that the group Otis Williams and the Distants had just signed a recording contract with Motown Records under their new name the Temptations.

Well, when I heard it through the grapevine, I was crushed. I could not believe that the same group I had practiced so long and so very hard with had finally gotten their big break without me.

Why minus me?

Again, if Motown's variety of "temptations" had happened overnight, then I "would of" been part of that original lineup. But because of several months' delay, I got caught up in another variety of "temptation."

With my "love supreme" now only a figment of some bygone yester-me, yester-her, yesterday, being the sixteen-year old man that I was did not physically permit the grass of puberty to grow silently under my feet or anywhere else. Michigan was the Cereal Capital of the world, and Battle Creek was not that far removed from Detroit. So, a street-smart romantic like myself had a whole lot of wild oats that needed boxing.

In other words, the bed I made with my girl required a "between the sheets" presence only an Isley-type brother could appreciate!

If only Berry's call would have come the next day, the next week, or within the next month, perhaps my body, mind, and soul would have been more preoccupied with Motown instead of them "mo' better blues" an untimely pregnancy often brings.

When my girl Shirley hit me with the "guess what," I felt the only honorable thing to do was follow the advice of the Silhouettes 1958 numero uno chartbuster and get a job.

Being the product of a broken home, I could not stand the idea of a child of mine being introduced to a world of fatherly abandonment and neglect. Leaving Shirley to make it all alone as a single mother was not an option for consideration.

Even though the Grammy award–winning "Papa Was a Rolling Stone" was more than a decade away, God had obviously impressed me that there would be no more symbolic "third days of September" intimately associated with my life. Subsequently, I quit Otis Williams and the Distants to support my baby-to-be mama.

A nest egg had to be built on something other than straw hope. Otis, Melvin, Al, Peewee, and I were absolutely clueless when opportunity would come a knock, knock, knocking.

I did what I felt a man any age had to do. I walked away from the group. I was willing to lie in the bed I had made with Shirley. The only problem, the word *lie* has a double meaning.

Shirley wasn't pregnant. She lied!

Yes, I left the group for what I thought to be the greatest love of all. The love of a would-be father for his unborn child. The love of a young man for a young girl whom he felt he had put in quadruple jeopardy. That's right: social, psychological, spiritual, and perhaps even medical.

But Shirley made her own bed, and she literally "lied" on it. And after finding out the truth, at that particular moment in time, I couldn't help but feel that she had ruined my entire life.

When David Ruffin left the Tempts for a solo career and broke out with the smash hit "My Whole World Ended," that's exactly how I felt. Shirley just might as well have placed a gun to my head.

As I struggled to remain the positive person I was always taught to be, I was determined not to allow my loss to affect the joy I felt for my friends. I was very happy for them. My total support went out to them for finally achieving the dream we had desperately sought.

So what happens to my dream deferred? Does it dry up and wither like a raisin in the sun? Well, there are dreams, and there are dreams. And my dream of being a Motown artist was too wet with my sweat to go bone dry.

Even though Shirley had committed the unpardonable sin in the book of my life, I was not going to let what I considered a modern-day Delilah zap my strength. If anything, I was determined to be stronger. I didn't know God then as well as I know him now, but he was with me. He had to be in order for me to survive that heartbreaking experience.

But again, it just goes to show the goodness and the greatness of a Savior that is willing to look out for you, even though you might not be looking out for him.

Does time heal all wounds?

No.

It took me about ten years to officially become a Temptation!
Do I hold that fact against Shirley?

No.

Since it takes two to tangle, the love my ex-girl and I shared
for all those moments was found on a two-way street. And since
the name of this "street" is Richard, I'll always see two ways of
looking at the situation.

You see (breaking it down), my first name embodies the
word *rich* as well as the word *hard*. And sometimes "doing the
right thing" is a "hard street" that will not make you "rich" in a
material sense.

Missing out on the dream of being an original Temptation is
the price I paid for entering into temptation. The fact that missing
out was the result of a lie does not make the price I paid any more or
less expensive. Had Shirley actually been pregnant, I still wouldn't
have been entitled to any psychological refund. Absolutely nothing
would have changed my fate. Richard Street still wouldn't have
been known as an original 1960–1969 Temptation.

I did what I had to do because it was the right thing to do.
And if I had it all to do over again, would I have done the same?
Well no!

I'd have marched Delilah's butt right down to the
neighborhood clinic and made damn well sure there were two
hearts beating in her body instead of just one!

Obviously, not having a dad or father figure in the house placed
me in at a serious disadvantage with regard to the psychology of
women from a man's perspective. I guess you could say I wasn't
thinking like a man; I was acting solely like a woman!

I was doing what I thought my mother would want me to do.
If I got a girl pregnant, it is my responsibility to take care of her
until death do us part. Yes, you go all the way down the aisle. You
jump the broomstick backward and forward until you get it right.

In being the fatherless man that I thought I was, it never once entered my sixteen-year-old mind that the girl I loved would tell me a lie. I mean not even once did it dawn across the horizon of my knucklehead that me as a "playa" was being played. After all, I loved her, and she loved me, and that's the way it was gonna' be: united.

But rather than a tune taken from the songbook of Peaches and Herb, somebody's herb is what I had to have been smoking!

Should of.

Would of.

Could of.

Let's look at this thing in reverse order. Could I have been an original Temptation? The answer, of course, is yes. I was there with Otis and company from jump-street as Richard Street.

Would I have been an original Temptation? The answer, in all probability, is yes. Barring any acts of God or acts of the devil, I don't see any reason why I wouldn't have been in the original mix. After all, in Berry's mind, I was in the mix that was being called back to ink a Motown contract.

Should I have been an original Temptation? The answer, honestly, is no.

God Almighty has 20/20 foresight. God knew from jump-street, despite Richard Street, that David Ruffin was going to be the man. It was not only David's voice, but it was also David's persona that made the Temptations' the household name we as a Motown group were to become.

Now, I'm an Indiana Jones fan. But I can't imagine anyone other than Harrison Ford as Indiana. Did you know that Tom Selleck (*Magnum P.I.* and *Blue Bloods*) was the first choice for the gig—not Harrison?

Tom Selleck is one of my favorite all time. Nevertheless, I ain't feeling Tom acting as Indiana Jones. And I just can't get to Harrison Ford as a Honolulu private eye rolling around the island in a red Ferrari.

No diff from a movie or a TV show, when I look back at who made the cut as far as the Temptations, I can't second-guess the Creator's master plan. It worked. God knew from jump-street, despite Richard Street, that the original lineup of David Ruffin, Eddie Kendricks, Melvin Franklin, Paul Williams, and Otis Williams was going to work big time.

Of course, I would have liked to have seen myself in that original stir, but who would I have replaced on that fabulous five-man team?

Backing into that thought, a song like "My Girl" was penned with a voice like David's in mind. The same applies to tunes such as "Since I Lost My Baby," "I Wish It Would Rain," "Ain't Too Proud to Beg," "Beauty's Only Skin Deep," and all of the other hits that found David out front.

Now, even over the course of time I found myself singing those songs as the lead vocalist, my voice is not a carbon of David Ruffin's. Only God will ever know the result of a world audience's reception if any voice other than David's would have had the same world audience result.

Certainly, the same holds true for songs like "Hey Girl" and "Heavenly" that found me out front. I'd like to think that I brought something unique to those two hits that could certainly be imitated, but not quite duplicated.

Keeping it real, it was that original lineup of David, Eddie, Melvin, Paul, and Otis that worked so well, it paved the way for me to officially join the team when I did. And, of course, for that I am, and will always and forever be, eternally thankful.

"O the depth of the riches both of the wisdom and knowledge of God! How unsearchable are his judgments, and his ways past finding out!"

THE MANNA OF MOTOWN

The year 1964 brought on a new beginning for me. With the Temptations now on the threshold of blowing up, I could either drown in the depths of personal despair or rise above the vicissitudes of inner anguish. I decided to "keep my head to the sky."

Ever hear of a group called the Monitors?

What about a song called "Greetings, This is Uncle Sam"?

Well, if you have or haven't, the Monitors was a group that I formed. And it is my voice that's heard greeting you on behalf of America's favorite uncle.

So just as it's written "to everything there is a season, and a time to every purpose," it was finally my time to get. And get is what I got. I now had me a group, a smash hit, and a job at Motown Records as a quality control manager.

What does a quality control manager do?

Well, it was my duty to listen to every song that was recorded at Motown. It was my responsibility to render both my personal and professional opinion with regard to clarity, style, and perfection. In other words, I was getting paid to do what all of us are most of the time willing to do for free. That is, rate a record!

However, instead of critiquing songs played on the radio, I was seated right there in the studio with my thumbs all poised to turn up or down at the slightest unflattering crack of a voice.

I was working right beside all the great Motown writers and producers. Before you heard such songs as "My Girl" and "I Heard It Through the Grapevine," yours truly heard it first. If it didn't get past me, it didn't get no ways near you.

How on earth did I wind up getting such a phat gig after being so down and out as described in the previous chapter?

Well, after the group went on without me, I really began feeling sorry for myself. I mean there I sat. No girl. No baby's daddy? No run-around pals. No nothing. I felt like my life was one big disappointment. I felt so low that now I was the one who had to look up to see the bottom. I'm here to tell you that I was singing, "Na na na na / Na na na na. Hey hey hey, good-bye," way before that group Steam!

I had even forgotten all of the positive things my mother had taught me over the years. I guess it was a damn good thing this was the early sixties rather than the late nineties. Because tragically speaking, if I had known anything about rock cocaine, I probably would have been a prime candidate for the crackhead hall of fame.

I didn't give a Rhett Butler damn about anyone or anything including myself. I felt my golden opportunity was "gone with the wind." I was pissed off at the world in general and me in particular. Like a seriously overplayed record, my soul had a deep scratch that mentally managed to keep reverberating, "You sure are stupid / You sure are stupid / A real damn fool / A real damn fool!"

But I'm also here to tell you firsthand that no matter how down in the dumps you may get, there's somebody up there who has an arm long enough to reach you if you really want to be reached.

You see, it was during my season of one-hundred-proof discontent that I had one of those experiences that make you wanna "go tell it on the mountain."

Of course, you've heard the saying that "it's always darkest right before the dawn"? Well, in one of my midnight hours, as I was going about my janitorial duties of diligently scraping dried crap off of a toilet in some downtown Detroit nightclub, I began thinking about the music career I loved and all the things that were and weren't happening in my life.

As I scraped and mopped yellow stains, I finally began to accept the realization that my singing days were over at the ripe old age of twenty-one. I finally began to settle the idea in my heart that it was time to move on with my street life—life without any realistic thoughts of a career in music.

As I scraped and mopped and flushed, I began thinking out loud about all the things I could do rather than sing. And then suddenly, out of nowhere, I heard a voice say, "Don't give up."

Somewhat startled, I immediately looked around to see who was there in the restroom with me. There wasn't; I was all alone.

Thinking someone was playing a trick on me, I went outside the restroom door, but there was absolutely no one in the long, darkened, and doorless hallway. I shook my head and started to laugh. I remember saying something to the effect that "now I'm even losing my mind (up in here)!"

As I continued working, even more frustrated than I was previously, I heard the voice again, sterner and more serious than before: "*Don't give up!*"

This time there was no mistaking. The voice came from an unseen source right there inside of that room. I guess you could say that it literally scared the crap I'd been scrapping right on out of me!

After hearing this voice for the second time, it was all I needed to rekindle the faith I had lost.

Now, almost fifty-something years later, there's no question in my mind that my ears were "touched by an angel." Right there in that restroom, amid the stench of human excretory waste, the

God of heaven sent a message to me. Yes, indeed, God is good. But allow me to expand on the moral of that story.

At the age of twenty-one, there I was scrapping crap off of a john. How far I had fallen! It was in a john that I had gotten my big break. Now, here I was in a john psychologically, emotionally, and spiritually broken.

Just check out the symbolism. Consider the irony.

But if you know anything about God in concept, theory, or firsthand actuality, that's how divine intervention customarily operates. That's God's MO (modus operandi) sort of speak.

When those three, or however many, wise men came a-calling, Jesus in a manger is not what they expected to find.

When Elisha sent a message to that dude Naaman telling him to go dip seven times in the Jordan River, Naaman pretty much said, "C'mon, man." Telling Naaman to take it to the Jordan is like telling Donald Trump to go see the pastor who does store front preachin' on the corner of Souls and Ville in Anywhere, USA.

And when Joshua ordered his boyz to march around the walls of Jericho doing a Tower of Power/Earth, Wind, and Fire number with their horns, you better believe there were some in the army who looked at Joshua sideways.

"Is you crazy?"

"What you been drinking, Josh?"

"C'mon, man, you 'bout to get us killed!"

The wise men were amazed. Naaman was healed. And the walls of Jericho came tumbling down.

The bottom line when you're on the bottom is this: The proverbial Red Sea can be parted in a place that's when and where it's least expected. As far as why and how, sometimes it's not ours to go figure. Most times it just is what it is because Jesus is who he is.

When I flushed the toilet in that john, symbolically that rush of water twirling around in the bowl was my Red Sea parting. I didn't have to hear that voice telling me "don't give up" a third time.

Twice was enough. My mother had always schooled us about not hardening our heart when we heard that "still, small voice."

The "still, small voice" I heard was telling me something that found me clueless at the time to fully figure out. Looking back, look at what I would have missed if I had allowed my hopes and dreams to have been flushed with the crap I was scrapping.

Not long after that epitome of an epiphany, my long-held dreams at last began to come true. I wasn't a Temptation, but I was working with them as well as with Smokey Robinson and the Miracles, Stevie Wonder, Mary Wells, Martha and the Vandellas, the Marvelettes, the Supremes, Marvin Gaye, and of course, Diana Ross.

And along with Warren Harris, Maurice Fagen, and Sandra Fagen, I was "greeting" the world as the lead singer of the Monitors!

Yes, I had evidently heard the voice of a heavenly messenger. And by the grace of God, I was wise enough to take some serious heed. Without a doubt, the 1960s was like manna from heaven as far as me and my Motown chart-breaking family were concerned.

Now, I could take the opportunity right here to "tell all" about what I and everybody else did and didn't, since I was deep into the mix. I mean, I shared the excitement of the motor town Motown Revue. I was right there on the bus with Marvin, Diana, Smokey, Stevie, Martha, Mary, Tammi, the Tempts, the Four Tops, the Contours, Jackie Wilson, and a host of others.

But, again, this book is not that kind of party.

I'll just suffice it to say that we were all young, gifted, and black young adults. And we did all the things that young, gifted, and black young adults do. So "just let your imagination run away with you!"

We had us a ball that wasn't confusing. When you're young and excited, there's a certain naïveté that goes along for the ride. It's like the innocence you carry on that first date. You don't think about whether or not that girl or guy that's holding your hand is a certified fool. You are just blindly willing to let the good times roll. And you're just myopically willing to roll right or wrong along with them.

Whenever I'm asked about "this and that" or about "so and so," I customarily try to provide an insight that's not rooted in rumor or fact that you can read in anyone else's book. Most of the times I tend to plead the fifth. What happens on the bus stays on the bus.

For example, my most-often-asked question is, "How was Marvin?"

Well, Marvin was da man. Despite all "this, that, and the other" that's been written and said, Marvin Gaye was an extremely talented brother. His silky smooth speaking and singing voice had an edge that would melt a female right smack dab in her seat.

If it's not already a core collection of your musical library, go out and get the classic "What's Going On." Listen to the lyrics and the musical compositions. They're all as current now as they were back then in the seventies.

And with further respect of Marvin's talents, there's the soundtrack *Trouble Man.*

On the back of the album or CD, it says, "Produced by Marvin Gaye—All selections written by Marvin Gaye."

"What's Going On" *Trouble Man* is my answer to any question asked about my good friend Marvin.

Then there was that light-skinned, green-eyed young man named Smokey Robinson. Unquestionably, one of the most musically gifted individuals to ever walk the planet.

> Just like the desert shows a thirsty man,
> A green oasis where there's only sand.
> You lured me into something I should have dodged.
> The love I saw in you was just a mirage?

I mean Smoke could lyrically take you from Venus and Mars to the Sahara. The man has a poetic range that is unrestricted by neither time nor space.

And since youth does spring eternal, little Stevie Wonder will always be remembered as the "giant" he's become. "Everybody say yeah!"

So when additionally considering the Four Tops Jr. Walker & the All Stars, the Isley Brothers, the rest of the Miracles, writer/producers Brian Holland, Lamont Dozier, Edward Holland Jr., Norman Whitfield, Barrett Strong, Marvin Tarplin, Frank Wilson, Harvey Fuqua, Johnny Bristol, Nickolas Ashford, and of course, Berry Gordy Jr. (not even mentioning the Tempts!) the talent pool was an ocean!

With all due respect to Motown's first few singer/writer/producer ladies, the men listed above were the bomb. They were the literal manna of Motown.

And strictly because *I didn't give up*, these were the men and women whom God blessed me with the privilege and pleasure of standing among.

In the deepest, darkest, depths of my despair, the power, love, and grace of God, through Jesus lifted me up.

Why?

Well, in reflecting, just maybe it had a little something to do with me doing what I believed was the right and honorable thing to do when it came to my not-so-pregnant girlfriend Shirley.

Just because it is written that "God is not the author of confusion," and I was definitely confused, God was just not going to write the final chapter of my life with me at age twenty-one. I was rewarded in God's own time, perhaps only because I chose to be a "do-right man" in the face of "my girl" choosing to be a do-wrong woman.

When hit with the news flash, "I'm pregnant," instead of saying, "What are you gonna do?" I made it a "we." I acted like the man God wanted me to be.

When God told Abraham to sacrifice his son, old Abe could have said, "I don't think so." Instead, he got to steppin' with knife in hand. From our here and now God perspective, we know of a certainty that the God we serve was not going to allow Abraham to kill his kid in the end. But from Abraham's in the moment perspective, no way Abe had a clue where the God he thought he knew was coming from.

The bottom line: There are tests of faith as well as tests of character. And more often than not, it's only through successfully passing those individual character tests that our individual faith in the absolute power of God is perfected.

God knew my girl Shirley wasn't pregnant, just as he knew he wasn't going to allow Abraham to kill his one and only boy. But because it was a test for Abraham, just as it was a test for me, God is not about the business of playing games with individual lives.

The God I read about in the KJV doesn't administer a test where folks pass it, and yet fail. God didn't reward Abraham with a pat on the back go back to business as usual. Rather, Abraham not only lived long, but he also prospered.

In a somewhat similar sense, I passed a test of sorts. And the grace of God that passes all my understanding allowed me to get back in stride again.

> Out of the night that covers me,
> Black as the pit from pole to pole,
> I thank whatever gods may be
> For my unconquerable soul.
> In the fell clutch of circumstance
> I have not winced nor cried aloud.
> Under the bludgeonings of chance
> My head is bloody, but unbowed.
> Beyond this place of wrath and tears
> Looms but the Horror of the shade,
> And yet the menace of the years
> Finds and shall find me unafraid.
> It matters not how strait the gate,
> How charged with punishments the scroll,
> I am the master of my fate:
> I am the captain of my soul.

"Invictus" by William Ernest Henley is one of my favorites. If I was going to sample a poem for potential lyrical "quality control" this would be the one.

For sure, I *am* the master of my fate, and I *am* the captain of my soul. Just like Moses in Exodus 3:14, the voice I heard sho'nuff told me so.

THE RUFF SIDE
OF THE MOUNTAIN

Some people say that the Temptations reached the top of the mountain during the sixties. I don't happen to agree with that opinion. And the fact that I didn't officially become a Tempt until 1971 has nothing to do with my opposition to what "some people" say or tend to think.

You see, if the Temptations had reached their peak in the sixties, then there would have been "nowhere to run to baby" but *down*! But contrary to a proverbial going south, the group kept right on keeping on in an uptown Saturday night northerly direction.

For example, "Just My Imagination" was released January 14, 1971, and topped both the pop and R & B charts at number one. "Papa Was a Rollin' Stone," released September 28, 1972, was a number 1 pop and a number 5 R & B as well as that latter category's Grammy Award–winning Song of the Year!

Remember "Masterpiece"? Well, it came smokin' down the track February 1, 1973, and checked in as an R & B number 1 and as a pop number 7. And how about "Hey Girl," the song in which I soloed as lead? It was introduced July 24, 1973, and climbed the R & B charts to number 2!

So I say all of that to say that it's invalid to believe a group has "peaked" if it's still seen to be climbing to heights it previously hasn't reached. And it's this continual upward mobility that's made the Temptations so phenomenal.

Just consider how badd the Chicago Bulls would have been if they could have kept on keeping on without Michael Jordan, Scotty Pippen and Dennis Rodman? What if they would have comeback the very next year minus that threesome and won the NBA finals?

You know as well as I do that when MJ, Scotty, and Dennis left the windy city, not just some people, but everybody said, "The party's over." And, of course, they were right. Even with a rose by the name of Derrick, you don't get a ring for just making the NBA Playoffs.

But as our story as well as history shows, that was not the case with the Temptations. There was no A team and B team thing going on here. When a member of the Tempts timed out, there was a player in the dressing room all suited up who was ready, willing and able to get in the game and score.

Motown may have thrown us a ball of confusion, but it was a ball that the music game's "fabulous five" never dropped. You see, in order to be a Temptation, "you had to have game!"

In 1964, Eldridge "Al" Bryant had game. But the operative word here is *had*.

Of course, as previously mentioned, Al was a member of the group Otis Williams and the Distants. He became a Temptation when Otis and Company signed with Motown.

Al was a humorous, quiet, soft-spoken kind of guy. Best person you'd ever want to meet if he didn't have any alcohol in him. But give him a few drinks, and his whole personality would flip.

An incident I personally witnessed that's illustrative of Al's wine induced mood swings involved him and Melvin Franklin. One day we were all standing around talking. Then suddenly, without warning, Al gets pissed about something as seemingly insignificant as how many ants live in an anthill. The next thing we know, Al picks Melvin up and drops him head-first into a trash can.

Being a lifelong fan of the Three Stooges, I had seen that stunt at least a thousand times. So, needless to say, I and the rest of the fellas thought Melvin head-first with longlegs dangling from a trash barrel was bust-your-gut funny. After all, Al was laughing harder than we were. The only problem, however, was Melvin. He wasn't laughing. He was hollering for help. And when we got him out of the can, the serious and stunned expression on his face said it all. That's when we realized there was something going on with Al that required serious consideration.

In Psychology 101 it's called an "aha" experience. It's when something hits you like a ton of bricks and you make a connection that you should have made a month or two earlier. I'm talking about that sudden realization that would make Arsenio Hall place his forefinger on the side of his head and go "hmmm."

You see, that wasn't the first time Al was seen to trip for no apparent reason. There was a time previous that Al hit fellow Temptation member Paul Williams in the face with a wine bottle.

Yes, back in the day the brothas drank wine. We drank it straight from the standard-size 750 ml bottle. Matter of fact, the real OGs called the wine we drunk "white port lemon juice." And those 750 ml bottles were as hard as a rock.

If by accident you dropped the brown paper bag that was tailor-made to fit the bottle, the paper would tear, and the sidewalk cement you dropped it on would chip without so much as even denting or cracking the bottle.

So, you see, being hit in the face with a back-in-the-day wine bottle isn't really all that funny. And the connection just wasn't made until the trash can episode that Al's temper combined with white port and lemon juice didn't mix outside the 750 ml bottle!

Now, I don't bring all of this up to cast a negative shadow on the memory of Al Bryant as an "original" original Temptation.

I'm just setting the stage for how one of the most recognizable names of all times became a member of the group. You see, unfortunately for Al, it was shortly after the trash can episode that he became the first of what would be many singers to leave the Temptations.

Anyway, during the first few months of 1964, Otis Williams approached me regarding Al's situation. Due to the great friendship I then had with Otis, and always enjoyed with Melvin, I was asked who I thought could fill Al's shoes. Of course, what Otis was really asking was if I wanted to come back with the group.

Well, at that time, I was the lead singer for the Monitors. And I knew Otis didn't want to come right out and ask me to quit my group. Believe it or not, one thing we all had back in the day that many have lost through the years is something called integrity. Or maybe you could just call it competitive values spelled L-O-Y-A-L-T-Y.

You see, unless you happened to have a crystal ball, nobody really knew who was going to blow up overnight. Because talent was so prolific, today's wannabe could wake up as tomorrow's superstar. In other words, if you were down with a group, you just didn't shelve your boyz or gyrlz for the hope of making it with somebody else. You believed in the fellas and ladies you were harmonizing with. And they believed in you. As a group, you stuck it out through the thick and the thin. Just because your ship hadn't come in by noontide didn't mean that it was never going to be seen sailing in the direction of your port.

We righteously believed that if you impatiently ditched your group in favor of another, sooner than later the trade winds of good fortune would somehow find that group you left behind. And one day there you'd be, wishin' and a hopin' you had stayed, but out there all alone by yourself.

In 1964, there was no way I could leave the Monitors for the Temptations. So I suggested David Ruffin replace Eldridge "Al" Bryant.

Excuse me while I clear my throat, and repeat that again.

I suggested David Ruffin replace Eldridge "Al" Bryant. So in reality I wouldn't have been replacing David Ruffin if I had played the cards that were shuffled and dealt me. In actuality, I would have been replacing Eldridge "Al" Bryant.

But instead of playing what was dealt, I went for the kitty. And, of course, the card kitty in this case was the four cards called the Monitors.

Taking my suggestion, David was hired. Remember, I was the quality-control manager for Motown Hitsville, USA. And if anybody knew talent when they heard it, that was me.

Now what can I tell you about David Ruffin that you haven't already seen, heard, or read for yourself? He was definitely a different kind of person. He kept to himself. He told none of his business. For a long time, group members didn't even know he had an older brother named Jimmy. (It was Jimmy Ruffin who had the monster smash "What Becomes of the Broken Hearted.")

The bottom line, with David there was no in between. There were no shades of gray. David was an individual you either loved or hated. But once on stage, you could only love him. He was the consummate artist—the performer's performer.

Even though I was a non-Temptation during those sixties years, the Tempts were my best friends. We all hung out together. So when I talk about any of the fellas, it's from firsthand, first-eye, and first-ear experience.

Now, due to the fact that David was already an established artist when he joined the Temptations, stardom was nothing to him. He took it all in stride. He would always give the audience his best, and the audience would show the entire group their appreciation.

Back to the sports analogy, you can talk stuff on and off the court when you are able to produce. However, when your stuff stinks, that's when you need to keep your mouth shut. David Ruffin could produce. So he was more than qualified to ride around any man or woman's town in his very own limousine that was monogrammed with a replica of his trademark glasses. Folks loved him!

If the news media had followed the Temptations like they followed the Beatles, you'd have seen women screaming, fainting, and flinging panties upon the stage too! The man was something else. So it wasn't about David being on an ego trip, but it was just about David being the eccentric kind of star that he was.

Eccentric?

Well, David was the kind of black man who would have never made it to America on the Amistad or any other slave ship. You know the type: an "I don't give a damn, ain't gonna take no mess from anybody" kind of individual.

Again, as we were accustomed to say back in the day, "if you gonna talk the talk, you gotta walk the walk." David was more than willing to walk it by going there with anybody. David was not too proud to beg the pardon of anyone, two, three, or four that interrupted his flow.

Remember that old commercial about E. F. Hutton? Well, when David Ruffin spoke, everybody tried to listen?

Tried to listen?

Well, every time David talked, he wasn't quite understood because of the dialect of his speech. In other words, the brother had a form of Ebonics that would blow an elementary school teacher away. David talked so fast absolutely no one could quite understand exactly what he was saying. And after every third sentence, he would laugh and say, "I don't have to take that mess from nobody!" And I quite often found myself laughing and agreeing with him!

But inevitably, as history tends to repeat itself, during those late 1960', Otis once again came to me for advice on a replacement. This time it was David Ruffin who was leaving. The rumored reasons were drinking problems and unexplained personal problems that had gotten out of hand.

Of course, there has already been a whole lot written about the life and times of former Temptation, David Ruffin. There's nothing I care to substantially add or subtract from the accounts that are already part of the public domain.

My remembrance of the Ruffin, as he was prone to calling himself, is all good. I loved him as I would my own flesh and blood brother. He was both genuine and real.

If you were about business, the Ruffin was about being business with you. If you were down with the Ruffin on a personal note, he was down on a personal tip with you. But if you were out there flimflamming on the pretense of being about something you really weren't, that's when the Ruffin came at you sudden, if not always correct.

I guess it was David's zero tolerance for anybody's bull crap other than his own that made all the right people uncomfortable—namely Otis Williams and Berry Gordy. You see, David wouldn't let Otis play leader of the group.

According to David, Otis Williams and the Distants was part of the distant past. The genesis of the Tempts as OW and the D was a rite of passage worthy of remembrance, not homage in the mind of the Ruffin. The bottom line, the Ruffin wasn't going to stroke Otis's ego. And just like Otis' initials: OW! That hurt! David was a pain in Otis's posterior.

Unquestionably, one of the great mysteries of human nature revolves around the issue of egotistical pride. Since David's voice was the lead on many, if not most, of the Temptations' hits during that time, there was understandably a public perception that David was the leader of the group. After all, when it came to television, radio, newspaper, and magazine interviews, David was the most popular Tempt. When it came to media coverage, it was always, "Otis who?"

The cameras were all turned in the direction of David. When Dick Clark had a question, the microphone was put directly in front of David's mouth. When any reporter had a question for the group, the attention gravitated toward the Ruffin and not anywhere near Otis.

Needless, but necessary to say, Otis did not like the implication of being OW with the *W* standing for *who?* In spite of all of those 1960s Temptations' hits with David Ruffin and Eddie Kendricks out front, Otis wanted what he considered his just due too. Otis wanted some R-E-S-P-E-C-T as the face of the Temptations. Unfortunately, for Otis, that wasn't going to happen.

One of my all-time favorite quotes is offered by Clint Eastwood in the 1973 Dirty Harry movie *Magnum Force:* "A man's got to know his limitations."

For some illogical reason that would even cause *Star Trek's* Mr. Spock to raise an already-arched eyebrow, Otis couldn't quite get it as far as his own artistic limitations. No matter how many times you present yourself as leader of the pack to the fellas, the ladies still ain't going to be balling up their panties and throwing them in your direction.

Now, that's not to say you won't do some collateral damage as far as pulling a woman from over here or over there by the mere fact that you are a Temptation. But a weapon of mass destruction—that's something you simply ain't packing. That's particularly when it comes to the masses that were packing the auditoriums and arenas to see us perform our hits as a group.

So in terms of all us Temptations, the ego of Otis was simply off the chain. And when your ego is running rampant, you will never appreciate what you're getting if you're continually hung up on thoughts about what you haven't had. What you think is in the best interest of others is, in reality, twisted to only be in the best interest of yourself.

Otis was a member of the Temptations along with everybody else who had been a member of the group he organized as Otis Williams and the Distants. But when ego prompts an individual to oversupport their individual selves, the end game is usually The End for any who won't play.

David Ruffin was not going to play the Temptations as Otis Williams and the Distants' game. It was just not the Ruffin's stick to point the microphones, cameras, and fans in the direction of Otis when they were up in his face. It was either David Ruffin or Eddie Kendricks that everybody wanted to touch, talk to, and see. It simply wasn't Otis Williams.

But again, OW, as in ouch! That hurts when you just can't let go of the "distant" past!

Of course, Melvin didn't have a problem in letting go. And, according to Paul, any member of the group could be in the spotlight as long as the fans loved them some Temptin' Temptations, which meant everybody was getting paid! After all, as Al Jarreau might say, why should anyone have a crabs-in-a-bucket mentality if the rising stardom of one meant the shooting stardom of all four others?

But the celestial height directly connected with getting paid is not all that when pride and ego are a celestial black hole. No doubt about it, pride and ego are a hellacious combination. And they're particularly foolish in the face of a collective popularity that was transcending economic, social, and political barriers.

How tragically disappointing to all of us was the fact that even despite the OW, the DR (David Ruffin) himself could not even cure the pain that comes with our collectively being superstars. David Ruffin was a megastar who should have taken himself more serious by taking himself less seriously.

Just as Otis wanted to be all that he wasn't, David wanted to be all that he was plus more. In a sad way, both Otis and David were afflicted by the same bug: "egoitis."

It was not enough that people all over the world saw David Ruffin as the main Temptation." David wanted the visual perception of his "main-ness" confirmed in writing. The Ruffin wanted the group's name changed to David Ruffin and the Temptations. And obviously, no way Jose was that going to happen. If Otis had a problem with Otis Williams and the Distants being buried with him alive, having David's name in front of what was once Otis' group was tantamount to a living cremation.

David Ruffin, despite all that he meant to the Motown brand, had an ego too big for bigger egos to endure, much less simply ignore in the interest of a few million dollars more.

Again, when we use the term *soul* as in *soul music*, we are dealing with the spirit. When Marvin Gaye said, "If the spirit moves you, let me grove you," there's more to that line than what casually meets the eye or ear.

The music we made stirred some serious emotions. Bob Marley even said, "One good thing about music, when it hits you, you feel no pain."

Well, there is a flip side to that Marley record. The music we made not only stirred the emotions of the hearer, but it also had an emotional effect on the doer, which stranger than truth was quite often painful.

While the "hearers" of the music are strictly focused on feeling the mood, the "doers" of the music are strictly focused on feeling the business. From a strictly business perspective that got personal, David Ruffin got too big for the Motown pants Otis Williams and, ultimately, Berry Gordy wanted him to wear.

As doers, the soul music we did was done so well that principalities, powers, and forces in high places began to see David through a glass darkly. If the man was left alone or allowed to do what he does with just a wink, who knows how high up the rough side of the music mountain, the Ruffin might inevitably climb.

If you climb Mt. Everest and reach the top, the closer you are to the sun. And being that close to the sun, well, your image just might cast its shadow on all who live in the valley below.

Quoting Paul (not Paul Williams the Temptation, but Paul the Apostle), "Now the works of the flesh are evident: enmity, jealousy, rivalries, dissensions, divisions, envy."

If you check out Galatians 5:19–21, obviously there's a few more works that I left out. But you should get the big picture.

David's image was casting its shadow over all of the Motown family. Via the presence of David Ruffin, the Temptations had grown bigger than Motown. The Temptations were Motown.

"Like a snowball rolling down the side of a snow covered hill. It's growing."

"Like the rose bud blooming in the warmth of the summer. It's growing."

Every day the Temptations were growing a little more than the day before. The *Ed Sullivan Show*, *American Bandstand*, *Hullabaloo*, *Shindig*, even over there across the pond in Europe, the entertainment world wanted them some Temptations.

Otis who? Maybe the powers that be could deal with that. But Berry who? That was a horse of a different color.

David Ruffin was nobody's fool. Like all of us, he had been there, done that, and bought the T-shirt. If he was the man, he wasn't going to be the spook who sat by the door. Once the panties that were being thrown on stage during a Temptations performance began to exceed the numbers being collected by Smokey and the Miracles, the Ruffin knew what time it was in more ways than one.

Subsequently, David's ego became more evident; and it made the egos of those big ballers and shot callers in Motown's heavenly realm become more evident as well. Bottom line, there was just too much evidence against the Ruffin for him to stay in that corner the Mighty Dells were singing about.

When considering all the memorable tunes that realized David as lead vocalist—"My Girl," "It's Growing," "Since I Lost My Baby," "Ain't Too Proud to Beg," "My Baby," "You'll Lose a Precious Love," "Beauty Is Only Skin Deep," "(I Know) I'm Losing You," "All I Need," "(Loneliness Made Me Realize) It's You That I Need," "I Wish It Would Rain," "I Could Never Love Another (After Loving You)"—the Ruffin personified Motown's joy and pain as well as its sunshine, blue skies, and rain.

Putting the real in it, David was what any industry calls a "rainmaker." By definition, a rainmaker is any person who brings clients, money, or respect to an organization based solely on his or her association. Since this music thing ain't exactly rocket science, common sense suggested that David's rainmaking skills and abilities far exceeded the rumblings of his thunder. But instead of seeing the Ruffin as lightning in a bottle, Motown saw him as a threat.

Keeping the real in it, we all know what happens when any man becomes a threat.

HOT WINGS

When the call went out from Otis to me about a replacement for David Ruffin, I "smh'd." Obviously, I didn't have the capability to text message my feelings and thoughts, so shaking my head, with a few appropriately placed expletives, was best I could do.

Of course, we were neither shocked nor surprised by the call, but being the professionals we were, we all had enough business savvy to know that you don't cut off your nose despite your face. We were old-school enough to know that if it ain't broke, don't break it in order to justify having to fix it!

Even though Motown had talent galore, we knew where we stood with David Ruffin. The man was battle-tested to the tune of all the hits that we had with him. Replacing David was pushing an envelope that we collectively felt (with the exception of Otis) that really didn't need to be pushed.

Speaking of need, there was our hit single titled "(Loneliness Made Me Realize) It's You That I Need." One of the lyrics on the track plainly says, "Let your heart, let your heart be your guide, forget about your foolish pride."

"Needing" to say, I wanted to practice what we were preaching. David needed to chill with the hair-brained idea of the Tempts ever being prefixed with his name. And since everyone and their mama knew hell would freeze over first before that idea of David's would even realistically be considered, Otis needed to freeze his ego with regard to David's idea being given any serious thought by Motown management.

The bottom line, couldn't we all just get along!

But be that as it may, again, just like before, when Otis came to me for a suggestion on David Ruffin's replacement, I suggested someone other than myself due to my obligations with the Monitors. The someone else I suggested was Dennis Edwards.

I distinctly remember the first time I ever saw Dennis. He was singing with a group called the Contours. Dennis was one of the biggest singing dudes I had ever laid eyes on. He was six foot three and weighed over two hundred pounds.

Now, the trip part about Dennis was watching him dance. In other words, a Fred Astaire and/or Michael Jackson "dancing machine" he wasn't! But after joining the Temptations, with Paul in charge of the choreography, Dennis's two left feet began to move in a synchronized style.

Strangely, however, it seemed as if each time I gave a recommendation as to who Otis should hire, even though I really wanted to step in and take the job myself, he did as I suggested. Both David Ruffin and Dennis Edwards became Temptin' Temptations as a result of the seed I planted in Otis's brain.

Now, would Otis have selected David and Dennis despite of my yay or nay, I don't know. I do know Otis asked my opinion regarding "who," and I told him I thought David and later Dennis were the best men for the job.

Because I had the God-given gift of musical discernment, I knew talent whenever and wherever I heard it. Obviously, despite my dreams to once again sing with my friends, deep down in my heart I knew the voices of David and Dennis were the right stuff for the Temptations at that particular Motown moment in time. And, with hindsight always being 20/20, the world is witness that my foresight was right on time.

Once again, can you even begin to imagine anyone other than David out front on "My Girl"? Or another other than Dennis doing what he does on "Psychedelic Shack"?

But as the saying goes, chances do seem to go around. It's the law of the wheel. For me, a third chance came around during the latter months of 1968. This time, Otis approached me about finding a replacement for Paul Williams.

Paul wasn't doing well at all. Rumors were running rampant that Paul was completely out of control with the consumption of excessive amounts of alcohol. He was also suffering from some terrible personal problems.

As Otis waited for my suggestion regarding a replacement for Paul, this time I suggested myself. Needless to say, he was very surprised because I had never before suggested me.

Having spent over eight years with the Monitors, whose members now consisted of Warren Harris, Tommy Ridgeway, Herschel Hunter, and yours truly, I had gradually come to the conclusion that nothing big was going to happen as far as the group was concerned. I felt if I had turned down and away from this third query by Otis, the opportunity of me ever reuniting with my friends would never come again.

So Otis agreed and I finally became a Temptation—in name only!

However, during the time Otis came to me, instead of the normal five, there were only four Temptations performing. Paul was not officially out of the group; it was just that his problems were quite often so self-consuming they would prevent him from taking the stage.

You see, a professional singing group is similar to a professional sports team in many ways. Although in some respects, there are some very basic differences. For example, if a quarterback or pitcher can't take the field for medical reasons, they're immediately placed on the DL (the disabled list). If they can't get it together in a certain amount of time, chances are they'll get traded. With professional singers, if you got a problem that's keeping you from taking the stage, your problem is placed on the DL. That's the down low.

Now, back in the day *down low* meant something entirely different than it does here in the now. The term in the manner we applied it had nothing to do with sexual healing. So when I say Paul's problem was on the DL, all I'm saying is Motown covered Paul's alcoholism up.

Paul was an original Temptation. Unlike an athlete, he couldn't be traded. And his familiar face and recognizable voice just wouldn't permit him to be fired unless there was an absolute necessity.

It's also important to know and understand that Paul Williams was a team player. He was absolutely no threat to anyone other than himself. Besides, since Paul and Otis shared the same last name, having Paul in the group meant Otis got his last name said twice. In a strange way that only Sigmund Freud can quickly figure out, Paul's condition was tolerable, if not cool with Otis.

Let anyone else, namely David, show up for work drunk as a skunk, believe me, they would have been on that "midnight train to Georgia" with a one-way ticket to ride.

So what do you do with a professional singer who's been placed on the DL? You put them on stage anyway with another singer parked in the wings who's actually singing their parts!

As Paul attempted to move his mouth to the songs he was faintly hearing, I was on the side of the stage with a microphone in my hand trying to keep up with all of his vocal movements. I guess you could say we had us a serious lip-syncing thing going on. I mean, who was lip-syncing whom?

Was I lip-syncing Paul? Or was Paul lip-syncing me?

Of course, my few close friends who knew the deal said, "Richard, that's messed up," with *messed* spelled with the letter *F*.

In my heart, I agreed. Singing in the wings was definitely not something I wanted to brag about. But these were my friends. And they were now such a popular group; I did not want to let them or their reputation sink because of one individual's fault.

I was a team player too. I was willing to except the position of being a utility outfielder for team Motown's Temptations.

Literally, there I stood in the wings mimicking every sound Paul made or was supposed to be making. And while saving the credibility, the good name, and the good grace of the Temptations, I knew if someone wasn't there to fill in the missing gaps the show couldn't go on.

So as the months went on, I traveled with the group from sea to shining sea. I watched and listened night after night as the rest of the group sang on stage to repeated applause and standing ovations. Even though I wasn't out front to catch the roses, I could still feel them being thrown. Yes, I was proud to be a real Temptation even though none of those countless millions of cheering fans ever saw me.

Unfortunately, my excitement became less satisfying as I watched Paul deteriorate right before my eyes. His now uncontrollable drinking habit went from worse to worser. Personally, I felt Paul's drinking problem could have been helped. I know I tried to talk to him. Make suggestions. Be a friend. But Alcoholics Anonymous I just wasn't. The man needed professional help beyond any of the group member's individual capability.

Standing behind the scenes, in the wings, I never saw Motown management lift a finger to provide the type of assistance that could have saved this brotha's life. And I do mean brotha. You see, before Paul was a Temptation, he was a human being. All too often, we allow ourselves to define people by what they do instead of by what they are.

I distinctly remember my first time meeting Paul Williams. I guess you can consider Paul as a music industry unsung hero. Paul was singing at a Woodland Park club in the historical community of Idlewild, Michigan, just outside Detroit.

At the time of that first encounter, we were just kids relatively speaking. Because of that age thing, I couldn't get into the club to be seated at a table, so I was in a back room watching Paul croon through a peephole.

After Paul would mellifluously finish singing a tune or two, his job was to then carry out the garbage.

Yes, there were no silver spoons that any of us ate with prior to our collectively gracing the stages of New York's Apollo, Copacabana, Radio City Music Hall, or the Upper Deck at the Roostertail Club in Detroit. Carrying out garbage and cleaning up restrooms was the way it was for not only Paul and me but also for many famed artists and entertainers who were simultaneously able to see beyond a mop handle, a urinal, and an alley.

On *The Temptations in a Mellow Mood* CD album, Paul sings the lead on a tune entitled "Who Can I Turn to (When Nobody Needs Me)." That tune wasn't Paul's on-stage signature song, but I think it probably captured the essence of what he was going through at that particular time in his life as a Temptation.

Drawn from actions that always tend to speak louder than words, it appeared nobody needed Paul Williams to be anything other than a Temptation. And once he got to the point that a Temptation was no longer something that he could be, there was nobody for him to turn to as a plain ole human being.

When the name "Williams" became too big of an embarrassment for Otis to tolerate, it was then time for Paul to go.

This is the downside of the business. But perhaps it's the downside of any business that's based on the individual as being a marketable commodity. Again, if you are a pro athlete, you're as good as your last game. If you are an actor, you're as bankable as your last film. If you are a singer, you're as hot as your last song. And if you're also a singer with personal problems that severely interfere with your professionalism; you're useful until you become all used up.

Looking at Paul, I began to realize that my professional destiny lay within his downfall. This was definitely not something to brag about.

The pressures of seeing my friend, whom I could distinctly remember when, deteriorate in the fast lane were becoming too much for me to handle. I went to Otis and told him I was unhappy about the way things were going. Otis replied by telling me, "If you're not happy with the way things are going within the group, get out of the group! Go on back to singing with the Monitors or find something else to do."

Otis had successfully managed to get rid of David by capitalizing on Ruffin's outspoken manner. And now he was telling me if my mouth wasn't put in check, he would seize the opportunity to get rid of me too.

I felt like a buzzard circling its prey. I knew my destiny as a real Temptation was found in the misfortune of Paul. Was singing with the Tempts worth the humiliation of singing in the wings? Was there favor found in a vulture's eye view of a grown man slowly killing himself?

Go on YouTube and look at some of the photos of Paul Williams. Behind the smile, there's a certain sadness that time hasn't camouflaged or managed to erase.

Except for my friendship and love for my cousin Melvin, the price was far too much to pay. As a matter of fact, Eddie Kendricks came up to me my first week as a Temptation and said, "Richard Street, this gig with the Tempts is not all that you think it is. One day you'll find out what's really going on, and you're not going to like it at all!"

With David gone, Eddie Kendricks was now unreservedly in the limelight. But unlike the Ruffin, Eddie, with his Southern charm, was a soft-spoken take-no-stuff kind of guy. I'm talking about the kind of dude who just looks at you when you piss him off. And you know in your heart that the cold unemotional glare that's given ain't really the end of it.

Whereas David was in your face like a bull in a china shop, Eddie was the guy with the knives at the Hibachi restaurant and grill. Stay out of Eddie's way and let him do what he does, or get in his way, and wind up sliced and diced before you can even think about cutting him back.

However, be that as it may, not even Eddie Kendricks had diplomatic immunity from the Otis Williams chopping block. There was not any favored nation status or entitlement based on how many record sales your voice as lead vocalist sold. Eddie was not down with the handling of David Ruffin. Nor was he willing to stand idly, buying into the Motown managerial lack of treatment concerning his lifelong best friend and Birmingham, Alabama, homeboy Paul Williams.

Eddie Kendricks being who he was spoke volumes without saying a single word. Sometimes what you don't say speaks louder than what you do. Definitely, it has a way of making folks more psychologically uncomfortable.

Finally, I had begun to see exactly what Eddie was talking about. I began to understand why David Ruffin had split without a fight. I had even begun to put two plus two together as far Eddie wanting to leave the group for a shot at a solo career.

Reflecting on the opinion of some of my closest family and friends, I too had begun to open my own eyes and behold how seriously messed up everything really happened to be beyond the glee. And as a consequence, even I began to drift into the mind-set that all of the Temptations' heydays were now behind.

It was 1968. David Ruffin had left. Eddie Kendricks wanted out. Paul Williams was pickling his liver in alcohol. Martin Luther King Jr. had just been murdered. The streets of almost every major black metropolitan area were on fire. H. Rap Brown was calling Detroit destroyed. Bobby Kennedy had just been murdered. And there was me, standing patiently in the wings waiting for anyone not to show or someone to die.

It was an artistically trying and crying time to be an entertainer in general and a Temptation in particular. In body, mind, and soul we weren't even three-fifths of a man. The group to which I had always aspired membership had tragically become slave to a system where wax was king instead of cotton. And picking hits instead of cotton was the business that plantation called Motown was now all about. Instead of Rich, I had become Eli Whitney.

As Motown's quality control manager, my brand of cotton gin enabled Motown as "massa" to master mo better hit recordings than ever before. Unfortunately, the hits, not so unlike a whip, were on the backs of many multitalented individuals who were being financially compensated as if we were all slaves.

Reparations and royalties have a whole lot in common!

Have you heard the one that goes, "One monkey don't stop the show?" Well, Berry Gordy must have coined the phrase. In 1968 Detroit, just like the Marvelettes sang, there was too many fish in the sea for craziness on the part of one, two, or even three monkeys. There was simply no monopoly on do-wop anywhere in Hitsville, USA. If I didn't want to wait in the wings, there was somebody, somewhere who would.

Just like Otis said, I could either take it or leave it. So I hung despite my personal feelings and frustrations. Invariably though, my mind would always rewind to the voice I heard in that restroom: "Don't give up."

Here then is a classic example of how life can serve you a diet of "do-do" (do this and do that) with a demand that you not only eat it, but you also do so with a smile on your face.

Consequently, no matter how hot I got about what was going on around me, I was at a point in my life where being a Temptation in the wings was far better than being no Temptation at all.

There was neither smile nor frown on my face. And even though I wished it would rain, the tears of this clown could still be seen—even though I was behind the curtain sitting in a theater's dark and hot wings.

BUTTERFLIES AND BEES

For yours truly, membership in the Temptations was a dream come true. Yes, in the midst of all that heartache and pain, that ball of confusion, there was an indescribable joy. Maybe like the joy you felt in the company of your first romantic love.

For example, imagine the joy that high school guy gets when he finally hooks-up with that cheerleader for whom he's always had a thing.

Or imagine the high school girl whose fantasy just happens to be the varsity quarterback. To the starstruck, the mere idea of that cheerleader having bad breath or that quarterback being anything other than a hunk is ridiculous.

Unfortunately, not until the morning after does reality slap ridiculous in the face. Not only does that cheerleader have stank breath, but she also has a few other places that could use deodorizing. And with regard to that hunk of a boy, once one on one, he's really found out to be anything but.

In other words, you can't just go on appearances. What looks great on the outside looking in may be totally different when standing on the inside looking out. Yes, Eddie had schooled me to the fact that all was not well in Hitsville, USA. But at the time he pulled my coat, I was too caught up in the magic of the moment to see anything other than stars. And one big star happened to shoot across my path after a performance at the Aladdin Quarters in Cherry Hills, New Jersey.

On this night, Paul had himself together, but I still managed to find myself hidden backstage in the wings. Eddie Kendricks, without word or warning, just simply decided not to show up. So there I stood in the dark behind the curtains.

This was a memorable moment because it was that one that broke the camel's back. It was that "one more heartache" Marvin sings so well about.

I just couldn't understand it. I was brought into the mix on the count of Paul; that I had learned to deal with. But here I was "standing in the shadows of love" for Eddie who just happened to wake up on the wrong side of his bed that particular day.

I had had enough. I had settled it in my heart, instead of my mind, that after tonight, that was it. The line had been drawn in the sand. This was not a basketball team, and I was no longer going to silently accept the role of sixth man.

You see, it was like this. I was being pimped. I was caught up in the rapture of loving the Temptation image without the Temptation substance.

Now, yes, I am familiar with Hebrews 11: "Now faith is the substance of things hoped for, the evidence of things not seen." But standing backstage behind a moldy smelling curtain calling myself a Temptation was plenty evidence that I was being seen as a fool. And seeing me backstage behind a curtain singing didn't require X-ray vision; just a fine tuned ear, along with lip-eye coordination.

My eyes had been wide shut. I finally fell awake.

Borrowing from Etta James, it was an "at last" moment. At last I began to see me as the butt of an in-house Motown joke. So "unlike Pagliacci did," I was no longer going to keep my sadness hid—smiling in the public eye. The tears of this clown were going to be wiped bone dry.

What was happening here, I had naively permitted Motown to make me the X factor for the Temptations' franchise. Yes, folks, when you got bank to the tune of millions of dollars in record sales (any kind of sales), you are a franchise. And *franchise* is synonymous with *property*. And, in my case, synonymous should be spelled *sin* as opposed to *syn*.

The sin was in the fact that Richard Street backstage gave not only Paul but also every Temptation a license to take a vacation whenever and for whatever reason they wanted. Richard Street had become Easy Street for anyone in the group who wanted to literally phone it in for the evening performance.

Just think how easy life would be if you had someone who would do what you do as good as you do it, and you could still get the credit for it even when you don't show up at your place of employment.

Now what do you call that kind of working relationship? Who does it really work for—the worker?

Hold it! If you're thinking I was still getting paid, so what's the problem? Well, the devil is in the details, and I'll get to all that jazz later. Suffice it to say until later; contrary to popular belief, it's not all about the Benjamins when it comes to being an artist.

When you are an athlete, you want to play. If you've got game, you can't get no satisfaction just sitting on the bench.

The same applies to an actor. You can't break a leg if you can't walk out onto that stage.

And being a singer is no diff. If you can blow, you want the world to know!

Athletes, actors, singers—we are all performing artists. We entertain audiences. The object of our desire is the audience. One of the big differences between being an amateur and a professional is the object of your individual desire. If your desire is yourself, then you are going to be content singing in the shower. And if you can get paid for singing in the shower where it's basically all about entertaining yourself, then playing to and with yourself is your highest form of satisfaction.

However, when it comes to a true professional, an audience of one is never going to be enough. The professional wants the big stage, the spotlight, the cheer or jeer of the crowd.

Trust me, if you can't handle the jeer, you're not prepared to receive the cheer!

When Temptations sing "Get Ready," one of the most powerful lines in the tune happens to be "So, fee-fi-fo-fum / Look out baby / 'Cause here I come."

Now, who said that first? It wasn't Smokey or any member of the Temptations.

Well, it was the giant in "Jack and the Beanstalk" that's been remade as Jack the Giant Slayer!

The operative word of significance here is *giant*. Bottom line, if you are a professional, if you don't want to be a giant in the entertainment business, you're not going to see yourself as ever becoming a giant in the entertainment business.

When we sang, "Fee-fi-fo-fum / Look out baby / 'Cause here I come," we were all individually and collectively buying into the giant mentality it takes to be gigantic in the music biz.

Google the Temptations' *Gettin' Ready* vintage album and check out the cover. The photo is shot in a dressing room showing the group gettin' ready to hit the stage. As professionals, just like the words in the song, it's "look out baby 'cause here we come." The *baby*, of course, is the audience we love—the audience that all true professionals madly love and adore.

A professional secret is found in the fact that no amount of money can quench the thirst to play the big show when the object of your desire is the audience. If Motown had offered me a hundred times what I was being paid to sit backstage and do what I was doing, it just wouldn't have been enough for me professionally—and more so personally.

I am an entertainer. I am a performing artist. And I am a professional. I will be all three until the day I die.

Gathered together in the Aladdin Quarters Cherry Hills, New Jersey, dressing room immediately after the show that night was over, before I could open my mouth in order to tell the fellas my party was over, there was a quiet knock on the door.

It was none other than Muhammad Ali.

As the Champ walked around the room shaking everyone's hand and shadow boxing with Dennis, since they were similar in size, a strange look suddenly came over his face.

Melvin, in his characteristic deep voice, said, "What's wrong, Champ? You didn't pull a muscle, did you?"

The room then got quiet enough to hear a mouse pass gas. Every eye was fixed on Ali. The earth seemed to stand still for at least ten seconds.

You see, unknown to any of us, Muhammad Ali was as big a fan of ours as we were of his. So when the silence was finally broken, we were astounded at the observation Ali made.

In his characteristic hushed voice, style, and manner, the Champ looked each of us directly in the eye (like we were standing before him in the ring as an opponent) and said, "I thought I was the greatest, but y'all are even badder than me!"

Melvin said, "How's that, Champ?"

Muhammad replied, "Sitting out there in the audience, there were only four of you guys on stage. But I could have sworn I was hearing five voices! Y'all are badd!"

We all looked at one another for a moment and then everybody in the room busted out laughing. The Champ had discovered one of Motown's best-kept secrets!

In order to continue the conversation, the Champ invited us all over to his pad that night. Now here we were in the presence and awed by the presence of Muhammad Ali himself. And there he was, Muhammad Ali, in the presence and awed by the presence (so he said) of us, the Temptations.

"I'm the greatest boxer of all time," Ali said again. "And you guys are the greatest singing group of all time!"

What a moment that was for me. And I guess that just goes to show that when you don't give up, being down and out doesn't necessarily mean you're out for the count.

Being in the same ring with Muhammad Ali showed me that chances really do go round for round as long as you keep your head to the sky. The sky, of course, is symbolism for God. If you stay focused on the God of heaven, you've got yourself a fighting chance. Unquestionably, I saw the symbolism inherent in the evening as we playfully shadowboxed—kicking it with the Champ.

Muhammad Ali went on to say time and time again how proud he was of us. He said we were a group of black brothers who were a much-needed positive role model for black society.

During that 1968 era, racism ran rampant, and segregation was a fact of life in many parts of these here United States. The only thing that appeared to remain universally positive and unsullied by bigotry was music as an art. Indeed, Motown was the Sound of Young America. A Pepsi generation of red and yellow, brown, black, and white.

Yes, as big of stars as we were, there we sat with the greatest. According to the Champ, as big a star as he was, to him, the Temptations were even greater.

Yes, I know I am repeating myself. But I'm only reiterating because I want it understood by anyone reading who might not understand. Wherever you are and whatever your condition, a change for the better can come as early as your tomorrow.

You can only imagine how great we all felt. Not ego kind of great, but humble. Muhammad Ali was the most recognized face on the planet. And there he sat in the midst of us five dudes who came from the streets of Detroit.

Borrowing the Champs' "float like a butterfly and sting like a bee," I can certainly say that all of us were stung by Muhammad's grace, wit, sense of humor, and downright down to earthiness. I must admit all of us sitting there in the presence of the Champ had a serious case of butterflies!

Needless to say, I forgot all about my little problem. The proverbial line I had drawn in the sand, Muhammad Ali's encouraging presence had completely erased. We, as Temptations, were grown street-smart men, but the Champ had reawakened us as little kids.

Instead of seeing ourselves selfishly, for at least a Motown moment, we realized our musical calling was for an even higher purpose. We made folks smile. We made them feel good for a lifetime of Motown moments, perhaps when there was not a whole lot in life to really feel good about. We were role models, not because we wanted to be or had to be. We were just role models because we all were who we are.

Collectively, I guess it took a close encounter with someone bigger than the sum of our five-part harmony to make us realize that we were bigger than we had even dared to believe.

So it wasn't about David Ruffin being gone, Paul being an alcoholic, Eddie not showing up, or Richard Street singing but not being seen. It was about accepting the proposition that together, we were "badd" despite our individual hang-ups and shortcomings. And that fact alone made it all good.

Personally, I guess it was God's way of showing me that my standing in the shadows was not in vain unless I allowed myself to be overcome by vanity.

Supernaturally, I know it is the greatness of God that placed one of the greatest of men in our audience that Cherry Hills, New Jersey, night.

So, "fee-fi-fo-fum," Muhammad Ali was a giant then, and, of course, he always will be to me.

In the context of the fairy tale life the Temptations were living, I was a Jack who had to slay his own demons first, if the climb to the top of that beanstalk was going to be both professionally and personally successful.

Sometimes a butterfly has got to sting itself like a bee to see beauty that's found in the wings.

CAESAR SALAD

During a performance in San Francisco, I was finally scheduled to perform on stage. As I prepared to make my grand entrance as an official member of the temptin' Temptations, Otis kindly called me to the side and told me that Berry Gordy suddenly didn't want me to perform on stage with the group. The bottom line, I was still supposed to wing it.

To say I was cussing mad is an understatement. That final straw I'd been willing to lug had finally become a log. Every positive experience I had ever realized as a Temptation had to be milked to the very last drop. If enough was enough, this was over the top and into the realm of the absurd.

I was so mad about the situation; I didn't even ask Otis why. And Otis knew I was so mad about the situation, he didn't even attempt to explain why. I was on a roller coaster that was turning me every which way but loose. So if I wasn't going to fall out, the only thing left to do was hold tight to every ounce of respect, dignity, and sense of self-worth my mind could find.

I guess great experiences like the one with Ali made me refuse to allow myself to fall totally victim to bull crap. I knew others appreciated what I was doing, and that counted far more than what Berry Gordy Jr., Motown, or the Temps thought about me personally.

But always when things seem to be the most discouraging, that's when courage is tested the most. Rather predictably, it was during the trials and tribs of this period that I was first introduced to drugs.

I was in New York, and a guy came around the group with a foiled package. This package sparked my interest, so I asked, "What's that, and why is it shining like that in my eye?"

Even though time and time again I had heard preachers preach that the serpent Eve saw in the tree was all shiny and glistening, there I was asking, "What's that, and why is it shining like that in my eye?"

Instead of the guy telling me what it was, he opened up the foil and put some of its contents on a little plastic ice cream spoon. Then he placed the spoon in my face.

Would you believe the next words out of this guy's mouth was, "This right here will open up your eyes and make you wise"?

Now how Genesis 3:5–6 graphic did it need to get!

But by me not wanting to look like a dope in front of the fellas, I opened my mouth to the taste of this strange powder! And when I closed my mouth, I must have made the strangest expression because everybody around me began laughing. Of course, I didn't know what was so funny. When I asked, somebody yelled, "Rich! You're suppose to sniff the stuff, not eat it!"

So just like Adam and Eve in the Garden of Eden, my eyes (and mouth) had been opened. In this instance, however, the forbidden fruit was cocaine. Thank God, it just wasn't my thing.

During those days drugs were not very popular. The poison of preference was a seventy-nine–cent bottle of wine. If anyone did use drugs, they typically smoked marijuana. Only the heavily addicted used needles, popped pills, and/or snorted. My, my-my-my-my-my, how times have changed.

But even though I was still winging it, the early '70s found me more financially secure than I had ever been in my life. I mean, Stevie Wonder couldn't have put it any better. Thanks to a heavy tour schedule, "everything's alright, uptight, out of sight!" The Temptations were headlining every major city in America. And we were playing every major venue in each one of those cities.

So just like Novocain, getting paid also has a very unique way of numbing aches and pains. I was now able to help my family in a manner I'd never done before. And I guess it was this fact alone that showed me just how resilient ego can be in the final analysis.

As long as I was faithfully performing my duties as a Motown employee who happened to be heard and not seen, what did I really care? Just as I had said earlier, I was singing songs that advised others to "forget about foolish pride." Shouldn't I follow the advice being modulated from the inner sanctum of studio and stage?

Henceforth, my obscurity as a Tempt was no longer going to be a personal issue. I had put it in the hands of the Lord. And even though I was called upon to walk through the valley of the shadow of the off-stage curtain, I felt no evil. At least I didn't until I discovered an ugly little secret that made the backbreaking straw I was already lugging even heavier.

While backstage in the dressing room before a nightly show, Otis and Melvin were boasting about how much money they had received from one of their royalty checks. Dennis laughed because he had received the same. I was the only one in the group who hadn't. To my surprise, I was on a totally different contract than the rest of the fellas.

Initially, I had been told my contract was the same as everyone else's. But now I had discovered that all of that was a lie. Instead of parity, I had been given the same kind of contract that brand-new, untried, and untested Motown talent was accustomed to receiving. And, of course, this meant the money I was formerly so happy and satisfied to be receiving actually amounted to little of nothing when accorded a panoramic view.

Since I had been a member of the group before it became the Temptations and had been there from the get-go as a butt-covering safety net, I felt I should have at least been given some kind of equitable consideration. I mean even if there had been a royalty pay scale increase after a six-month or nine-month period, I could have worked with that. But that was not the case.

When I questioned Otis about the rest of my money and why my contract was different, I was viewed a troublemaker! I was given a lecture on how "grateful" I should be to be called a Temptation. I was even accused of trying to break up the group!

Now, when you stop to consider all of the songs the Temptations made during the '60s through the mid-'70s, we're not talking about royalties that amount to chump change. Today, if you turn on the radio, TV, rent, or buy a video, CD, DVD, surf YouTube, sooner or later, you're going to hear or see a Temptations' tune. And I'm talking about a Temptations' tune that was first heard back in the day, i.e., mid-'60s through the '70s. So with regard to royalties, we're talking serious money.

Unfortunately for all of us Temptations, Otis being the exception, the contracts that Motown got each of us to individually sign played all of us collectively as chumps. This either means we were all some stupid MFs (Michigan farmers), Otis being the exception, or Cain was really on to something when he asked the Lord in Genesis 4:9: "Am I my brother's keeper?"

Who wants to be a millionaire? Well, David Ruffin, Eddie Kendricks, Melvin Franklin, Paul Williams, Dennis Edwards, Damon Harris, and yours truly all should have been!

Remember that 1998 NBC miniseries (based on Otis's book) that supposedly told the truth about the Temptations? How much money do you think the Ruffin, Kendricks, Williams, and Franklin estates collectively collected from that national network presentation?

How much do you think any of the Temptations (other than Otis) who are still among the living received?

Not a dime!

The bottom line here is the bottom line. I just wanted to get my fair share of what was mine. I felt I should be paid for all of the hard work and effort I had contributed to the group. It wasn't anything personal. It was business—strictly.

I mean none of us should have had to give up that which rightfully belonged to us. We were the greatest American singing group of all time, yet we were being "hoodwinked and bamboozled" by an organization and individuals we considered to be our family and friends.

OW! It hurts.

Here is where the "ball" we were all having started to become "confusing."

However, here in a new millennium, some may say, "You guys were just stupid to allow yourselves to be taken advantage of like that. It's your own faults."

Yes, I guess, we were naive. I certainly didn't understand the business. I was simply overwhelmed by my newfound Detroit state of mind. I was too busy trying to be the best possible Tempt that I got caught up in the show, forgetting all about the business.

Everybody in the entertainment business has got to know that when your focus is entirely on the show, sooner than later you're going to get the business. And I'm not talking about getting it in any positive sense.

With the Monitors, the *M* could have stood for "Musketeers." With my old group, it was "One for All and All for One." With me and the Tempts, it was an entirely different story. The *M* standing for me with the Temptations might just as well stood for "Mousketeers." With the exception of Otis, we were dealt with like being members of the Mickey Mouse Club.

Unfortunately for us, we were young, and our stupidity with regard to business made us prime targets for getting advantage taken. But even though it is a new millennium, sometimes the more things change, the more they remain the same.

Back in my day, it was the young, gifted, and black who made Motown the music capital of the world and seated Berry Gordy Jr. as chief of state. Today, it's the young, gifted, and black who make hip-hop culture's rap an international empire with names like Master P, Diddy, Tupac, and B.I.G. firmly established as heads. Certainly, if historical repetitiveness can be realistically expected, tomorrow will also find the young, gifted, and black on the cutting edge of some other kind of musical phenomenon.

Therefore, in order to deal with show bizzness's need for greed and its obvious use and abuse of the young, gifted, and occasionally stupid, housecleaning has got to begin at home. The cobwebs, dirt, and dust of trust are best vacuumed by a clearly understood contract that dots all the i's and crosses all the t's when it comes to individual best interests.

With us Tempts as a whole (Otis included), it was just a situation of getting caught up in something so gigantic that you become a spoke in a wheel that has no spokesman.

While we wore all the stylish outfits and drove the big cars, those who wore the three-piece suits and rolled in either a Ford or Chevy lined their pockets with all the money.

Unfortunately, too many of us back then, and now, accept the proposition that threads and a bad ride are all the average brotha really wants anyway.

But Madison Avenue knew the deal. They knew the monetary value of the Tempts because they were profiting from our entire organization. And, in many cases, outsiders across the board were able to calculate what the Tempts were making because their groups were making much more, and they weren't nearly as popular.

But, nevertheless, at the time, I was an entertainer, not a doctor, lawyer, or an Indian chief. As far as I was concerned, since Otis was the self-proclaimed leader, when it came to my contract, I felt that he should have gone to Motown's president and/or lawyers and demanded the group be paid equally!

How stupid was me, myself, and I?

Again, we all came up together. We were brothas, and we were friends. But just like crawfish in a bucket, you already know that story's continuing saga.

"Am I my bother's keeper?"

"Nothing personal. Just business, my brotha!"

Or maybe even as Caesar dramatically put it in his famous last words, "Et tu, Brute?" Translated this second time around, "You too, Melvin?"

I guess I expected too much from a 'notha brotha from a 'notha mother. I mean the great expectations I had regarding my very own cousin, Melvin, began to show up shaky.

But let's put the sho'nuff for real in it. If you think enough of me not to stab me yourself, at least tell me there's somebody back there with a knife!

But then and again, perhaps I should have taken a page out of David Ruffin and Eddie Kendricks' notebook. Maybe I just should have barged into Berry Gordy's office on my own and politely asked him (with a couple of well-chosen adjectives in the forefront), "What is this mess!"

Not making such a move made me grieve from within. I realized that the same guys I thought were my family and friends were neither. They were only people looking out for themselves and not for those who had helped them become all they musically became.

I again tried to hold on to my pride, while holding on to my job by not rocking the boat. Even though my name is Street, I had forgotten the first law of the streets: "Do unto others before they can do unto you."

But an even mo' better approach to stopping the madness that comes with the territory is to just refrain from doing serious money business with family and friends. Seriously, you want to maintain a personal friendship? Avoid doing any business with that personal friend that involves money. When personal expectations exceed professional accountability, disappointment and hurt feelings are the result.

As tight as we Temptations all appeared to be, even though we were "standing on the top," we were also walking the edge. It's a terrible thing when trust becomes a four-letter word.

Unfortunately, when it comes to the entertainment business, a rule of thumb is you "trust no one." Doubly detestable, that also includes your own mother, father, sisters, and brothers.

Cliché is the comment that the moment someone even interjects trust into the conversation as an alternative to a legal contract, run the other way. Subsequently, a gentleman's agreement confirmed by a handshake to seal a deal is about as rare as a 1943 copper penny!

Just in case you didn't know, in '43 most of the pennies were silver in color. So if you've got a colored Abe Lincoln dated 1943, you can cash it with a coin collector for about $10,000.

I say all of that to say, in the music business, or perhaps any business, doing business solely on a promise to do the right thing is worth about as much as a red cent if the year is any other than 1943.

While there will always be exceptions to the rule when it comes to money and trusting in friends right along with God, motivation to do the wrong thing will always be a temptation.

I was a thirty-something Temptation. And I had just had the rude awakening that money and friends are a whole lot like vinegar and oil when it comes to making a salad. Unless shaken and stirred, the liquid ingredients don't naturally mix.

WATERGATED

It was 1972. Shortly after the discovery of my second-class citizenship, there was another personnel change among the ranks of the group. In addition to Dennis Edwards having replaced David Ruffin, Damon Harris had now replaced Eddie Kendricks So, the fabulous five were now Dennis Edwards, Damon Harris, Melvin Franklin, Otis Williams, and yours truly.

Our first album with me as an official member of the Tempts was titled *Solid Rock*. Just like the name, we, as a group, were solid as a rock.

But let me give you a little background on exactly how all of this, that, and the other came about. As far as Damon Harris, he literally walked off the street and into the Temptations.

I distinctly remember us doing this DC engagement. Dennis was now firmly entrenched in the role once occupied by the Ruffin and the fans loved him as much as they had his predecessor.

A new guy by the name of Ricky Owens had attempted to fill the shoes of Eddie Kendricks. But anybody who has ever been a Temptations' loyalist knows Eddie's footsteps are some extremely difficult ones to follow. Eddie, in his heyday with tunes like, "The Girl's Alright with Me," "The Way You Do the Things You Do," "Get Ready," "Girl (Why You Wanna Make Me Blue)," "Please Return Your Love to Me," "I'll Be in Trouble" had the golden voice that put the *wow* in many of those early smash hits.

I mean with that crystal clear, silky-smooth falsetto of his, on a bad day made worse by chronic chain smoking, in those postsixties later years, Eddie Kendricks couldn't even do Eddie Kendricks. At least not the Eddie Kendricks the world had grown and known.

But again, Eddie's departure was no surprise. Because of Motown managerial circumstances and situations that weren't going to find Eddie Kendricks laughing when it wasn't funny or scratching where it didn't itch, Eddie wasn't feeling Otis Williams or Berry Gordy, and neither of them was feeling him.

Gladys Knight & the Pips had a smash titled "It's Time to Go Now": "Arrivederci. Tally-ho. Au revoir. Adios. You've been so wonderful, I don't wish to go. But this completes my show."

Eddie's "bonsoir" to the Tempts is poetically illustrated in the lyrics of Gladys's song.

But again, just like I had previously said, Eddie did warn me early on that my fantasies concerning the glamorous life of being a Tempt might be in for a rude awakening. He was right. David Ruffin was now gone, and so was he.

Enough background. Back to the then future.

During this particular DC performance, when it came time to do the Kendricks's classic "Just My Imagination," Ricky Owens, the new guy, became shaken, rattled, and rolled up into a ball of nervous knots. Instead of saying, "Each day through my window I watch her as she passes by," Owens says, "Each window my day through."

Well, "Just My Imagination" strikes one of those kinds of grooves that compels the audience to sing along. Needless to say, as soon as buddy boy couldn't come correct out of the blocks, the boo birds started. And this was the very first time any of us Tempts (new, regular, original, and old) had ever been booed. As a group, we didn't know what a *boo* was. It was something remote we had only heard about. It was something that only happened to other performers. Not us!

Even though I was parked on a stool in my usual offstage perch as fill-in support for the alto harmony, every boo heard brought a pang as sharp as if I had experienced it firsthand.

As the chorus of boos sporadically continued, a young fella and his girlfriend sauntered up to me. The young man was Damon Harris. His first words were, "I can do that Eddie Kendricks's number as good Eddie."

Shocked by this little skinny dude's bodaciousness, the only thing I could say was, "You not supposed to be back here. Motown personnel only."

Unmoved by my official-sounding bark, Damon repeated himself verbatim. And before I could repeat myself verbatim, the number was concluded, and offstage walks the fellas with Dennis Edwards cursing mad. As a matter of fact, I thought to myself that as big as Dennis is, he didn't need to be getting that upset with anybody. If he had decided to punch Ricky, it would have taken Melvin and Otis, along with me, myself, and I to stop him. And both Melvin and Otis were now nowhere to be seen. So it would have only been the three a-ME-gos to intervene.

Still cussing, Dennis looked directly at me and said, "I'll never go on stage with that guy again!" And for some inexplicable reason, the only thing I could say was, "Here's a guy who says he can sing as well as Eddie."

Dennis didn't even look at Damon. With his back to both of us as he walked away, his only comment was, "Have him meet us at the hotel after the show."

Well, since it was at that particular time, 1971, I turned to Damon and asked him if he'd ever heard of the Watergate Hotel. He said he hadn't, but he thought he could find it.

The rest is history. Damon, along with the entire world, found the Watergate before "all the president's men." Damon walked into a suite full of party people, and blew the crowd away. To some folks, Damon Harris is accused of doing Eddie Kendricks better than Eddie Kendricks!

With Dennis and Damon now planted firmly in the mix, it was almost like David and Eddie were part of a very far-away distant past. I think Damon's vocal abilities caught all of Motown by surprise. The staunchest Temptations' fan was challenged to distinguish between Damon and Eddie. There were even some in the public domain that didn't even know Eddie Kendricks had left!

So as further testimony of the group's greatness, the hits kept on coming. Just like a 440 relay team, the '60s handed the baton to the '70s. And "Superstar" led the way to "Papa Was a Rollin' Stone," "Masterpiece," "Hey Girl," "Let Your Hair Down," and "Shakey Ground."

Between 1972–75, "Papa" reached number 1 on the pop charts. "Masterpiece," "Let Your Hair Down," and "Shakey Ground" all hit number 1 on the R & B with "Hey Girl" peaking at number 2. Along with Dennis and Damon, I was credited as a lead vocal on "Superstar,: the Grammy Award–winning "Papa Was a Rollin' Stone," and "Masterpiece. " On the ballad "Hey Girl (I Like Your Style)," I was the solo lead vocalist.

After three years with a three-fifths entirely different staff, the Temptations had already made their mark. But my extreme displeasure at discovering I had been lied to as far as my contract was too bitter a pill to merely close my eyes and swallow.

During a local TV interview in one of the cities where we were performing, I lashed out at Berry Gordy. I felt my contractual constraints were his entire fault.

Keep in mind, when I became an official member of the group, I was no stranger to the Motown family. I had been the organization's quality control man. I had even played big brother to Berry's little kids during those early days. So it wasn't like I came to dinner with a lot of false expectations with regard to hospitality.

How would you feel if a friend thought enough of you to trust you with his or her kids, but not enough to trust you with an umbrella when it's raining? Viewing the big picture, a contract ensuring my royalty rights was as significant to Motown as a pimple on the butt of a camel. I mean other than maybe the camel, who in the world would really give a Rhett Butt-ler?

Certainly my entitlement to royalties as a senior member of the Motown family was not going to break Motown's treasury. If bull crap flows downhill like lava from the mouth of a volcano, then yes, I blamed Berry.

Understand, for a recording artist, royalties are analogous to a savings account where you never make a deposit. You're just continually drawing interest. If you've got product somewhere out there in the world that's still drawing the public's interest, that product is still generating financial "interest" from that record, CD, or DVD buying public.

Bottom line, you should be getting a piece of the action in the form of a regularly scheduled check. Depending on the popularity of that product to which your name is attached (along with your particular lifestyle), you could live off of royalties from here to eternity. Public popularity that rises to the height of a Michael Jackson, Paul McCartney, Elvis Presley could guarantee economic security to the second, third, or maybe even fourth generation of descendants.

So my being ticked about royalties wasn't some Shakespeare much ado about nothing. Again, today, right now, this minute, every time you hear a Temptation tune somewhere in the world, somebody in the world is getting paid. Unfortunately, it's not the family members of any one of the dead or living who once-called themselves the Temptations circa the '60s to mid-'70s.

Now during the early to mid-'70s, I was still financially secure, but the security only came as long as I was on the road performing. Unlike the other members who were getting royalty checks, when I wasn't working, I wasn't monetarily situated. This meant even as a Tempt, I was only about a half dozen performances away from being down and out in Beverly Hills—destitute and broke.

You see, being an entertainer back in the day placed certain psychological demands on your paycheck. For example, if you were a Tempt, you couldn't wheel around town in a Ford Focus if there had been such a thing.

If you were a Tempt, a shirt, suit, or shoe that bore a K-Mart, Wal-Mart, Target, Sears, JC Penny, or some sort of discount label was definitely "foe paw." (That means unfit for a dog's foot!) I mean, Men's Warehouse couldn't guarantee jack for a temptin' Temptation.

If it was a wristwatch, it was a Rolex. If it was a house, it had to have a swimming pool. If it was tickets, they had to be for seats close enough to see the performer sweat. And if it sparkled, it better be a diamond! There were just certain expectations you didn't want to get around even if you could.

Whose fault is it that us entertainers have been programmed to feed such lavish and extravagant tastes? By necessity, I have to plead the fifth.

But as unfortunate as it is, in this society, to be a celebrity that the public will pay to see, it costs money to maintain a celebrity status.

Let's put the real in it. If Denzel Washington moved into the so-called hood, folks would be impressed for about a minute. But once the novelty wears off (probably after about a month), the rap would suddenly be, "That you know what ain't you know what."

Now, let's look at the fickle in that. This brotha who you used to pay big bucks to see on the big screen has suddenly become "not all that."

Why?

Because he now lives next door to you!

So what does that say about you?

Back in the day, as well as today, fans expected their role models to be "all that" and more. I mean, who wants to look up to somebody they have to look down on?

Remember that tune we sang about "Don't Let the Joneses Get You Down"? Well, the message in the music was for our profit just as much as it was for the listening public! Relatively speaking, if you're functioning off of a "Whopper with cheese" salary, a champagne, and caviar wish list can only be realized through credit.

Before me or any of us knew it, royalties or not, the checks were spent before they even hit the bank. Heard of direct deposit? Well, all of us had direct debit! Subsequently, for us, missing one show was like an everyday person missing a whole month of work.

If you're on a tightly balanced budget, can you imagine what one or two months without pay would do to your physical welfare and mental state of mind?

After that TV interview where I put Berry on blast, Otis hit the ceiling with Melvin following right behind. They couldn't believe I said all of the bad things I did about Motown and "Mr. Gordy."

Now everybody had known Berry for over a decade, and both Otis and Melvin were still calling him "Mr. Berry." I'm talking about in private conversations just among ourselves! They didn't want to take the permissible liberty of being on a first-name basis with "the boss" even when it came to kicking it with the fellas. I mean these two "birds" gave the term *brown-nosing* a whole new meaning.

Whatever the case, news about my disenchantment traveled fast. But I didn't give a damn. The only thing I felt was right. "Right as rain," the Stylistics might say.

Just like Popeye the Sailor Man, "I'd done took all I could stands, and I can't stands no more!"

I mean David Ruffin had called Mr. Gordy a "Michigan farmer" both to his face and in public over a contractual dispute.

And prior to Eddie Kendricks's leaving the group, he had told Berry to kiss his ass and had publicly questioned Mr. Gordy's sexual relationship with Diana Ross.

Unquestionably, in view of the Ruffin and soft-spoken Eddie's antics, what I did was rather mild in comparison. Nevertheless, I did expect to be fired.

But I had my self-respect. At that moment, despite bills, debt, fame, and fortune, nothing else mattered. If a man or woman is raped and pillaged of their self-worth, no amount of money can buy it back. My ass-kissing days of getting along just to keep a job were at an all-time end. I was prepared to take my talents elsewhere. Anyplace where they would be fully appreciated I was willing to go.

To my complete shock and utter surprise, Berry didn't react to my allegations. He didn't blow his top. He didn't say a mumbling word. As I grew older and wiser, I realized just why silence is golden. Berry had nothing to say because he was not guilty of the accusations I had leveled against him. Berry didn't have anything to do with my contract. It was all Otis. Otis was the MF (Michigan farmer) in the mix.

Again, OW! That hurt.

You see, it was Otis who told me one thing and then hand-carried the direct opposite someplace else. And even though Berry didn't immediately modify my contract to make it all good, my respect for Mr. Berry Gordy was nevertheless restored.

The flip side of this script, however, taught me a very important lesson that I've never forgotten. Sometimes you've just got to maintain your cool until you've gathered all the facts. I had bowed to the pressures of my family and friends who told me I was a fool and Berry was the culprit. I listened to my heart instead of my head.

Well, that whole ordeal reminded me of that story you've all probably heard about the little bird.

I'm talking about that bird who ran into a snowstorm while flying south for the winter. What it was, this little bird's wings iced up causing him to crash-land in a gated barnyard.

Lying there in the snow all frozen and about to die, a cow comes along and craps all over this little bird's head. So in addition to being almost frozen to death, the little bird is now buried beneath some foul, stank cow manure.

Certain more so now than ever that it's the end, the little bird begins to say his prayers for the very last time. But rather than curtains, the warmth from being covered in all that foul, stank cow manure gradually begins to thaw the little bird out.

Feeling blood flow throughout his wings and entire body, the little bird starts to sing and chirp loudly for assistance. The little bird feels he desperately needs to be rescued from underneath all of this cow crap.

Aroused by all of the commotion, along comes a barnyard cat. The cat slowly investigates and then swiftly digs the little bird out.

Happy ending?

No. The cat immediately proceeds to gobble this little singing bird up.

The moral of the story?

Everybody who craps on you ain't your enemy. And everybody who gets you out of crap ain't your friend. And if you are warm and happy in a pile of crap, you better keep your big mouth shut until you see for yourself, just who is who.

Unfortunately, smothered in the midst of my crappy contract, I discovered there were a whole bunch of happy little birds singing away in Motown's gated barnyard.

ROUTE 66

In 1974, I had made a move. Motown had motored west two years earlier, so, California, here I come to join other group members who were already there.

Before I made this move, I had asked Otis why the entire group needed to relocate. After all, we didn't have to motor west. There were daily flights from Detroit to LA. And having a West Coast studio flat was just as practical.

But to the contrary, Otis wanted everyone in the group to be closer to Mr. Gordy. He said the company was there, he was there, and if I wanted to keep my job, I'd better be there too! So "Got to Be There" was the song Otis had us singing right along with Michael Jackson.

First off, I really couldn't understand making this move because it was going to be very, very costly. Second, I really couldn't understand why those of us who wanted to stay in Detroit couldn't. Detroit was home, and home is where the heart was, so this Route 66 decision as it pertained to the performing artists just didn't make any sense—to me.

But, like I said in the last chapter, there were a whole lot of "birds" flying around Motown who didn't want to get "iced." And I personally knew unless I was really prepared to leave the nest, I was wise to keep my bird mouth shut.

I mean, David Ruffin flew the coop and wound up landing somewhere in the land of Nod. Sure, he had a couple of smash singles, but as a solo artist he never achieved the success that was expected.

And Eddie Kendricks, even with his solo albums *All By Myself*, *Keep On Truckin'*, and *Boogie Down*, he still wound up flying across that musical Bermuda Triangle. Compared to his celebrity persona as a Temptation, he was really never heard from again.

Actually, outside of Diana, Smokey, and Michael, nobody venturing too far astray the group roost has ever managed or been managed to achieve any major stature of solo success.

For example, remember the name William "Bill" Griffin?

Well, he was Smokey Robinson's replacement with the Miracles. After a few hits with Pete Moore, Ronnie White, and Bobby Rogers he decided to go solo. Obviously, today his identity would be a great game show question! Maybe even one of those end-of-the-show *Double Jeopardy* questions.

And, what do you know about Jean Terrell? Have any ideas what her claim to initial fame happens to be?

Well, she was Diana Ross's replacement with respect to the Supremes. She tried to wing it in 1978 with her first album. Again, her name is another great question guaranteed to stump "whoever wanted to be a millionaire"!

So, awareness of such Motown trivia explains why so many of us went along with company cow crap. Most of us were warm even if we weren't all that happy. I know I didn't want to move to LA. But I didn't want to get caught in any Michigan snowstorms either!

By moving from Detroit to Los Angeles, everything was higher. I mean taxes were higher. The cost of living was higher. Since most of our gigs were east of the Mississippi, transportation expenses were higher.

Actually, the cost of living had doubled and even tripled what it was in Michigan. For example, in circa 1974 Michigan, a person could buy a nice house in a nice neighborhood for $70,000. But in the Fresh Prince's neighborhood (Bel Air) that same style of house cost at least $270,000!

Ask me how I know?

Well, according to Otis, this is what Mr. Gordy wanted. We were Temptations, and by virtue of being a Temptation we were expected to represent success.

And besides, we were from Detroit. We didn't know the diff between Bel Air and Compton! Most of us had been in Michigan all our natural lives. By not knowing anything about California, we accepted the proposition that living in this area would be conducive to industry business. So again, we did as we were told.

Two or three performances not only covered the monthly mortgage, but it also took care of the Rolls or that Magnum PI style Ferrari. Like I said before, we had what was called "direct debit." Motown took care of everything.

If a wife needed a new dress or a pair of shoes for the baby, all she had to do is call it in. If the toaster stopped its pop, all she had to do is drive by a designated appliance store and pick another one up. She told management what she wanted, and they responded with what they felt both of you needed. And this is exactly how many of us could live in a quarter-million-dollar crib with only a few hundred dollars in the bank or back pocket.

Since we were all part of a well-known, top 10, chart-busting group, Motown felt we shouldn't have to worry about the cost of California's inflation or anything else. And, of course, that anything else included our money.

The sad fact was all of us bought into that Taurus scatology. I mean it didn't dawn on us that since the company paid for everything, the company owned everything. Everything was in the company's name. And since the company was also the money managers, we really didn't know how much money we "managed" to make!

Looking back, most of us didn't see any difference between living like a millionaire and actually being one! I mean if you happened to be a single man like I happened to be, you were systematically programmed to live for the moment and not for the future. The way we were rolling, The Temptations should have been singing "Living for the Weekend" instead of the O'Jays.

I mean it's very easy to get caught up in shadows that have no substance. A world of fame and just a little bit of fortune is a serious aphrodisiac. I mean every time I'd sing "Hey Girl (I Like Your Style)," there would be at least fifty girls only a phone call away in any given city who were "liking mine" as well.

So, economically, even though my contract was not equal to everyone else's, I was given just enough fringe benefits to stay socially, if not totally, appeased. You see, it's the "fringe" that keeps many entertainers living on the edge.

On a political front, this West Coast move pulled my coat to a whole new vibe. I discovered the "California black versus white" thing was more visual than the Detroit experience had ever been.

The white groups who played the West Coast were able to have concert sellouts in large stadium arenas. Many of these groups would gross salaries well over a million dollars per night. On the other hand, black groups, such as the Temptations, normally played exclusively to small auditoriums. This meant a sellout only grossed in the hundred-thousand-dollar ranges.

This factor of low-gross selling concerts also played a big part in the high-cost-of-living challenges all of us faced. So despite our individual contractual relationships with Motown, this thing of being head over heels in debt gradually began kicking everybody in the butt. I believe it's called trickle-down economics!

For example, the Midwest in general and Detroit in particular are blue-collar markets. You could count on "living for the weekend" to mean a Temptations concert. In 1974 California, however, "living for the weekend: could be Disneyland, the

Dodgers, the Rams, the beach, or a 1,001 other ways to live and die of happiness in LA.

Now given the fact that black families didn't realize the income levels of their Caucasian counterparts, when whites did their living and dying, they were more economically capable of doing so.

Strictly because of this harsh reality, black singing groups had to work harder just to survive and stay alive if they resided on the "left coast." With all of the socially entertaining diversions to compete against, they also had to work for longer periods of time in order to get comparable salaries. White singing groups only worked when it was convenient for them to do so.

Inherently, ivory was set up to succeed, while ebony was set up for failure. But in the case of us, rather than putting the blame totally on that white elephant, we rhinos became willing participants in our own oppression.

I mean management across the board went south once we pulled out of Detroit. Due to California laws, Motown was no longer able to manage any of its artists as it had previously done in Michigan. State regulations, corporate commerce, and a whole lot of legal jargon none of us really tried to understand required the group to seek professional counseling and managerial services elsewhere.

So by allowing ourselves to embrace ignorance of what was happening around us, Otis's hiring of an accountant by the name of Jerry Schwartz as well as the law offices of Ralph Salzer went uncontested. In consultation with Schwartz and Salzer, Otis made all group decisions without input from anybody else.

Subsequently, these decisions not only proved detrimental to my health and wealth, but they were also disastrous to the entire organization.

In 1974, I sang the lead to a song called "Heavenly." Due to what can only be classified as some stupid mess, the rising success of this song was abruptly halted. It mysteriously fell off the charts after only nine weeks of airplay.

Why?

Well, someone in Otis's managerial hierarchy instructed the Temptations to stay on the road and work rather than attend Dick Clark's first annual American Music Awards. That year we had been nominated Best Vocal Group of the Year.

When it came to making that important public appearance—a showing that could give additional creditability to a group's stature—we weren't even present. Rather than any one of us Tempts, Ewart Abner, then president of Motown Records, accepted the award on behalf of the group. He gave great thanks to Dick Clark, but not any of the disc jockeys!

As soon as we heard his speech, we knew there would be trouble. By Abner not giving credit to the DJs, every black radio station in the nation blackballed us. My lead song "Heavenly" and the follow-up Temptation tune "You've Got My Soul on Fire" were systematically dropped from station play lists all over the country.

And to make matters worse, the DJs also turned their backs on other Motown acts that were on the charts during the same time. Snubbing America's DJs for Dick Clark resulted in an economic downfall for the entire company. In a way you could say, Motown chose "Dick" and got screwed.

Now, the irony of this working rather than appearing decision was all about the Benjamins in the first place. Motown had been convinced by its management that revenues to be made in concert during the night of the Dick Clark thing were far more important than attending Dick Clark's thing. Needless to say, that myopic view cost the company millions in record sales.

But this kind of shoot-yourself-in-the-head approach to business management was nothing new. Another incident involved the NAACP Image Awards.

We were invited to perform during a time where there were absolutely no discernible scheduling conflicts. Of course, this NAACP event was an awards ceremony that needed our attendance for no other reason than a demonstration of support for the causes of black people.

Well, an Otis-handpicked manager by the name of Shelly Berger convinced him that the NAACP Image Awards conveyed the wrong image for the Tempts.

Indulge me while I say that one more time again. An Otis-handpicked manager by the name of Shelly Berger convinced him that the NAACP Image Awards conveyed the wrong image for the Tempts.

Absolutely amazing how a plain ole burger with positively no fixin's can suddenly replace the taste of the wholesome soul food that you grew up on. Otis was so far up Shelly Berger's assets that he couldn't see the difference between a debit and a credit. Showing at the NAACP Image Awards would have been a definite credit to the Motown family. But Otis and Shelly made our no-show a serious liability. According to Shelly, we were a crossover group.

In addition to losing money on a show night that he intended to book somewhere in America, a Temptations' appearance at an NAACP black affair might be a turn off to all the white American fans.

Now is that "white enough for you"?

Unfortunately, even though all of us (with the exception of Otis) knew this was the wrong thing to do, we were all individually too deep in debt to afford any mo' bull crap. We went along with Otis's decision to shove the NAACP Image Awards up Shelly Berger's you-know-what—the place where Shelly felt it belonged as far as the Temptations was concerned.

In the words of Malcolm X, Otis had been hoodwinked and bamboozled. And we had "Temptation walked" right along with him in the interest of going along with the show.

In the words of Malcolm again, "If you don't stand for something, you will fall for anything."

Well, we fell.

But isn't this the manner in which most celebrities and wannabes fall? God blesses us to go out and make a lot of a little money. Then the first thing we do is hire a manager or an agent or a wife or a husband who has absolutely no interest in us other than the money.

When Tina said, "What's Love Got to Do with It," she was trying to school you before you let somebody fool you. But there we go getting caught up in the rapture of an Anita Baker beat and don't see the forest until we're lost in the woods—as in Tiger if you catch my drift—as in wood, one more time again.

The sports and entertainment industry is full of $40-million dollar slaves as my man William C. Rhoden put it. But these chains and shackles are not wrapped around the wrists and ankles; they are fastened around the mind.

When Temptations sing "Take a Stroll Through Your Mind," we weren't kidding when we followed with "you'd be surprised at what you might find."

What we found was everybody's thoughts other than our own! Right along with "a mind being a terrible thing to waste," so is a whole lot of money.

When we did the "Reunion," there was another one of those "falling awake" moments that slaps you on the butt with a shoe as opposed to a hand.

David Ruffin being David Ruffin was sitting in a hotel restaurant with one of our road assistants. This roadie let it slip that all of us were supposed to be collecting something like $15,000 a performance instead of the $10,000 we were getting.

First off, why does this dude who does pretty much nothing but unload equipment and set up lighting and sound know anything about our financial business!

Second, there is a big difference between doing stupid and dumb things and being stupid and dumb. Most of the time when it comes to business, folks forget adding, subtracting, multiplying, and dividing is second-grade level. When grandma sent you to

Ball of Confusion

the store at seven years old to bring back a pack, you had better come back with the right stuff and the right change.

Third, the Ruffin wasn't a blunt instrument. Certainly not on this occasion; David had ordered prime rib. The knife he was holding had a jagged edge. Once the roadie realized he had made a slip, and then tried to make a slip, David was right behind him with a steak knife.

Needless but necessary to say, Temptation or not, a black man chasing a white man through a hotel lobby with a steak knife is going to draw attention.

When David was restrained by hotel security and escorted back up to our private floor, we all convened in Eddie's room to get the dirty lowdown.

That is, all of us but Otis convened in Eddie's room. Otis wasn't invited because the roadie had fessed up that it was the decision of Otis and Shelly Berger that $10,000 is all that we should get per performance.

Having the 411, we all marched down to Otis's suite to straighten it out. Of course, Otis did the Hollywood shuffle and pointed the finger at his pal Shelly. Cool Eddy simply said, "Well, let's get Shelly on the phone."

With a half dozen angry black men in the room, Otis did what was requested.

But now for that falling-awake moment, when Otis said, "Shelly, the fellas got a problem about the pay," for some inexplicable instinctive reason, my finger hit that button on the phone that instantaneously puts the party on the other end on speaker.

In Shelly's own words, "You tell those niggas that they are the show, and I am the business. They sing and dance. That's all they are supposed to do. They get what I decide to give them."

Hello to the hell no.

At least that's what we said. But talking loud and doing nothing was what we were all about. Again, when it's all about

145

the Benjamins, that's what you're all about. We weren't forty-million-dollar slaves, but we were $10,000-a-show slaves divided by seven. We allowed our individual and collective selves to be bought for $1,428.57 a gig; and that's before taxes.

So just look at what the glamorous life had made us all. And just like Curtis Mayfield sings on the 1972 Superfly soundtrack, "so you wanna be a junkie—wow."

Applied to my version of street life, so I wanted to be a Temptation—*wow*!

The *wow* here ain't superfluous. In other words, it ain't random. It implies disbelief at the self-inflicted degradation of the black community and just how low we will go.

Wow is a whole lot for a three-letter word.

An old wise man told me when I was playing that old folks home as a kid, "Son, a dollar never falls too low for somebody to pick it up."

He was right.

Wow.

But perhaps the biggest awards ceremony missed during the early '70s was the night of the Fifth Annual Grammy Awards. Instead of being at the Shrine Auditorium in Los Angeles, we were some 2,700 miles away. Crowded around a small, black-and-white TV in a Fort Lauderdale, Florida, motel, we watched Moms Mably accept our Grammy for R & B Song of the Year: "Papa Was a Rollin' Stone"!

So just like Papa, so was us Temptations. We weren't anywhere to be seen by family, friends, or fans. We were managerially too shiftless to even show up to receive our own Grammy. We weren't working. We weren't doing jack; we had just been managerially jacked. As a matter of fact, we were so organizationally trifling, no one representing Motown even bothered to show up. No Berry Gordy. No Ewart Abner. No nobody. The best we could do was a gravelly voiced comedienne of questionable gender who had been invited to appear as mere comic relief.

The greatest achievement of the Temptations to that date was that Grammy. And we had a granny—a 1970s version of Tyler Perry in drag—accepting our award. And due to conditions and circumstances we refused to control, one of our greatest accomplishments was made a joke.

In the face of all these scenarios, I once again became very down and out in Beverly Hills. In addition to the hot-under-the-collar reality of having a contract that provided no royalties, I also had to endure the hard, cold reality of a disorganized organization. I mean, how you corporately manage to forget the Grammy Awards when you've got a song nominated for Song of the Year, Satan in hell knows.

Also, in view of the way the organization was being conducted, I was troubled by the fact that if I should die while being a Temptation, my family would have been forced to take up a collection. In addition to no royalty rights, there were also no retirement plans or life insurance policies. I mean there was no group plans set up for any group members. Otis included.

Wow.

Now, indulge me while I say that one more time again. Otis included!

Wow!

Otis was playing us and being played at the same time. Motown became a West Coast plantation, and we were collectively nothing more than Kunta Kinte in patent leather shoes and stylish suits. Otis may have thought he was in the house, but he was a field Negro no different from anyone of us other four. We were all hoodwinked and bamboozled by the glitz and glamour of Hollywood.

Yes, indeed, the route we took from the motor city to LA was a real "trip." And, unfortunately for me as well as many others, the 66 that gave us our kicks began to look a lot like boxcars.

We had literally and figuratively crapped out.

THE THIRD COMING

Maybe it's just one of those things Michael wrote off as "Human Nature."

There I was looking out across an LA morning as the city's heart began to beat. Yeah, I was reaching out, trying to touch her shoulder. But at the same time, instead of California dreaming, I was still in Detroit. Hitsville USA.

Yeah, it was the dawn of a new day. Here I was on the left coast. But borrowing from Atlantic Starr, my heart wasn't in it. I was on the Pacific, but instead of it being all that and a bag of chips, I was "dreaming of the street" from whence I came. I was telling myself it was human nature for me to be thinking of the way I was.

Straight out of an Isley Brothers' songbook, this old heart of mine, which in reality was really very young, was reflecting on my good ole days with the Monitors.

Now what's wrong with that picture? Here I am—a member of the top R & B group in the land—and there I am mentally singing "Memories." I'm talking about those Barbara Streisand "memories of the way I were!"

Yes, Virginia, I know us Temptations did a tune titled "Memories." But my mind was stuck on Streisand. Them there memories of the way I was were all up in the corners of my mind.

I mean they were so misty and water-colored I could have quit the Temptations, joined the Dells, and sung a rainbow.

Yeah, that's the way I was.

If you don't know from experience, it's human nature to retreat to memories of the past as a psychological refuge or comfort zone for dealing with the present and what's believed to be the future. My mind had flashed back to the fun times I had in the company of my old group.

Maurice Fagin, Sandra "Candy" Fagin, Warren Harris, and I were the Monitors. With the Monitors, there were no "temptations" to think evil thoughts about anyone or anything. We were living the life we loved, and we were loving the life we lived.

We were all from Detroit, so the Lions, Tigers, Pistons, and Red Wings had nothing on us homies. We were a team too!

We didn't have to sleep with one eye open when we went to bed at night. We all individually and collectively knew we had each other's back, front, and both sides from head to toe.

Now, for those who may say, "Richard, you're trippin' to even be thinkin' that the good ole days with the Monitors can even begin to compare with what might be called bad ole days with the Tempts," well, I'm here, once again, to school ya before somebody fools ya: All that glitters ain't gold.

Yes, indeed, Jack climbed the beanstalk. But guarding the gold was a giant. Not even thinking about the fame that went along with the fortune, Jack returned and did it again three mo' times. Each and every time, buddy boy was fortunate to escape with his life.

Two times before, I was asked by Otis to give my opinion with regard to who would be best to fill a Temptations vacancy. By being quality control manager at Motown for a number of years, I had a well-tuned ear for talent. By being raised in a household where my mother taught us to be honest of heart and truthful, I gave an opinion I believed was in the best interest of both Motown and the group. For me, from where I sat at this particular time, the third coming with the question, "Who do you think?" and me naming myself, well, it wasn't the charm that I thought it was going to be. In a way, I was feeling like Jack must have felt not knowing the end from the beginning.

Jack no longer saw the gold coins, or the golden eggs. And as far as that magical harp, the only tune being played on it was "fee-fi-fo-fum." Jack had to have thought he was toast. That he was about to be that giant's English muffin!

And check out Peter. He even walked on water for a minute. But what happened when that disciple of Christ took his eyes off Jesus for a second? Yes, he began to sink.

Peter, in all likelihood, began to see and contemplate exactly where he was and what he was actually doing. Peter had left the comfort zone of his ship, which wasn't all that comfortable given the stormy weather wherein he found himself. But now he was seemingly worse off than he had been before.

True, with the Monitors, we never fully realized any gigantic claim to fame. Our most memorable hit, "Greetings (This is Uncle Sam)," was the closest we got to smash hit status, at number100 on Billboard's pop and number 21 on the R & B in 1966. But it was just like the saying that sometimes "less is more" when peace of mind is the preferred corner store.

Looking back, the main reason we as the Monitors didn't skyrocket the charts with a bullet was because of in-house politics that translated into in-house professional neglect. At the time, unfortunately for us, we were too much like the Miracles.

Smokey had Claudette. The Monitors had Candy. Additionally, there was also that light-skin thing going on as well. Remember, it was the early to mid-'60s, which meant "yellow is mellow."

Even though the 1966 Donovan classic "Mellow Yellow" was rumored to be about smoking dried banana skins, which was believed to be a 1960s hallucinogenic drug, black American pop culture understood "mellow yellow" in terms of skin complexion.

Bottom line, Motown was not going to corporately invest in any group that would publicly compete with Smokey Robinson, Claudette Robinson, Bobby Rogers, Pete Moore, and Ronnie White—a.k.a. the Miracles.

Richard Street, Maurice Fagin, Sandra Fagin, and Warren Harris—a.k.a. the Monitors—were just SOL, i.e., "so outta luck"! Two "mellow yellow" handsome dudes with a dark and lovely girl singer was one too many for Hitsville, USA, a.k.a. Motown.

It wasn't formalized in a Motown memo, but every MFSB (mother, father, sister, brother) working for the corporation knew that the best material in terms of tune and lyric was not going to go our way. If a house divided can't stand, a record company calling itself a "town" was definitely no exception.

Pun intended, it would have been a miracle for the Monitors to have been elevated in a manner comparable to Smokey and his group. That's not a knock on Motown and the accomplishments of Smokey Robinson; it's just a revelation respecting the nature of the music industry as a business first and foremost.

I know the saying "It's nothing personal, just business" is cliché, but when it comes to the entertainment business, it just is what it is. If you can't stand the stress or strain of rejection for no other reason than just simply being told, "I ain't feeling you," then you better get yourself a gig stacking boxes on a rack or books on a shelf.

We all knew what time it was in terms of the career decisions that were being made, as well as those that would have to be made. Whether one likes it or not, it just doesn't make good business sense to divide your external market by creating internal rivalry. For example, we "Heard it Through the Grapevine" from Gladys Knight and the Pips before we "Heard it Through the Grapevine" from Marvin Gaye.

Even though "Grapevine" was a smash for Gladys and Marvin, it would have been promotionally insane to release the same title track by both artists simultaneously. Even though the buying public loved Gladys and Marvin, it was not in Motown's business interest to pit Gladys against Marvin in terms of vying for national record sales.

Marvin couldn't be a stubborn kind of fella when it came to marketing and promotions. He had to patiently wait his turn, or literally be doggone.

Likewise, with Smokey in the house, I, too, was going to have to patiently wait mine. That is, if I was going to be all I could be under the Motown banner, brand, and label.

So, just like the apostle, I took my eyes off Jesus too. I began to reflect and reconsider the move I had made with regard to joining the Temptations. Even though my personal income turned from hundreds to thousands of dollars overnight, I couldn't get no satisfaction.

Having been an all-state athlete in high school, organized sports had provided me with a work ethic that I brought to the Temptations. Just being a Temptation just wasn't good enough. I had to be the best Temptation ever. If a rehearsal was called for ten o'clock in the morning, I was going to be there in the studio at nine thirty locked and loaded—ready to roll.

For me, being a Tempt was a job first, as much as being a privilege and pleasure. There was no hanging out or going to parties from dusk until dawn. Singing with the Monitors for eight years taught me to be a leader. So by being the leader in my group, I had high expectations of what a leader should be and do in other groups.

Because to me, it was ideally about one for all and all for one, I had expected Otis as the self-proclaimed leader to lead by example. The group had to be front and center stage since there was no one individual name preceding the Temptations as such was the case with the Miracles, the Supremes, the Pips, the Vandellas, the Vancouvers, and the All Stars.

News flash: This was by no means the case in the case of the Tempts. The Otis Williams golden rule is this: "It's all about the Benjamins. And you can call me Ben."

Subsequently, it was so sad for all the rest of us who could not see beyond the bling bling of the moment. We all bought into the hype. Otis, as Motown mouthpiece, sold us the sizzle. We looked good, we sounded good, and we smelled the aroma of success good. Not until we began the taste test did we discover that the beef was missing. And, of course, when it came down to me asking, "Where's the beef?" that's when the troubles first began.

Because we were who we were, who were we to question anything management did? The Temptations were the show; Motown was the business just as Shelly Berger had said in no uncertain terms. Once you move on up from a Big Mac and fries to Steak and Lobster, with a dash of caviar as an appetizer, the managerial opinion is prevalent that you best keep your mouth shut if you want to dine. The elevator that takes you up has an arrow that also points down.

Since all of us as Temptations were now walking on water, far removed from the Detroit streets, the attitude of Otis, who had the ear of Berry was, "what's the problem."

It was the position of Otis that for anyone who didn't want to go along with the program, "let the door hit you where the good Lord split you."

After all, for Dennis Edwards, Damon Harris, and I to get in, we had to fit in the vacancies created by David Ruffin, Eddie Kendricks, and Paul Williams. And Otis was always ready to remind us of that fact.

So just like the name of our first album minus Tempts' originals David, Eddie, and Paul, we all were operating on the self-delusion that we were standing on "solid rock." The "rock" we were on, however, just wasn't the Rock of Ages. It was the fourteen-carat variety.

It was a house in Hollywood Hills.

It was a car right off the showroom floor in Beverly Hills.

Illustrative just how easy it is to get caught up; I distinctly remember the first car I bought as a Tempt. It was a powder-blue Ford Galaxy. I was a star, and being a star meant I had to be among other stars.

And where do stars live?

A galaxy, of course!

As fate would have it, Melvin tore up my Galaxy arguing with his wife. I didn't have my ride for a week before it lost its brand-new undented luster. Even though Melvin willingly took care of the repair costs, there was an object lesson to be learned.

And what was the moral of that story?

Don't put your mental health in material wealth!

I guess that's why "In God We Trust" is printed on the back of a dollar. It's engraved there to remind us that a bag of gold coins, hens that lay golden eggs, and harps—no matter how magical—are all temporary. They don't and won't survive earth, wind, fire, or a man simply arguing with his wife when it's your car he's driving.

Because hindsight is 20/20, if I had kept the faith by maintaining my focus in trusting God as opposed to a buck, sweet dreams would have replaced my sleepless nights. I would have embraced the physical and mental approach that "God's got this." I would have thereby let go and let God as the saying goes.

I would have eliminated the negative by accentuating the positive despite circumstance and appearance to the contrary. Instead of sinking in the depths of despair, our *Solid Rock* album title would have been more that an album title by providing us a firm foundation on which we could individually, collectively, and confidently stand. Certainly, my decision to leave the Monitors after that third coming of Otis asking for my opinion would not have been second-guessed.

But singing in the wings as an unofficial Temptation for six solid-as-a-rock months had an effect. In my mind, I was already a Temptation. Little did I know what I had thought all the time was just a bad case of my imagination running away with me.

Without rhyme or reason, one day out of the blue I get one of those BTW (by the way) news flashes that my membership in the Temptations is probationary. I was told by Otis that I had to prove myself.

Yes, I hit the roof without a ladder!

I mean, hadn't I already proven myself? I felt, along with everyone else in the group, with the exception of Otis, that doing what I did behind the curtains for the last half year had already proven myself. For Otis to tell me that I would be on probation for a year was an outright insult.

I wasn't the guy who was chauffeuring the Temptations. I was seated in the limo with them. But how easily we selectively forget when we have a selfish spirit and not-so-hidden agenda.

But the moral of the story, even though I wasn't a rookie out of nowhere when it came to singing, I was a real nowhere man when it came to the fine print on a recording contract. I allowed my own self to be raped and pillaged by signing a no-royalty contract for a few dollars more than I had made singing in the wings.

If you're thinking, "Wow! I didn't know Berry Gordy was like that." Well, Berry Gordy wasn't like that. Leave the front end *W* off the *wow* and you got *ow*. This was the gospel according to Otis Williams. Berry had no idea about what was going on. The contract relationships involving the group members were Otis Williams's rules.

I had stood my ground backstage in the wings at practically every one of the major venues wherein the Temptations sang, so it was a slap in my face for someone I had always considered a friend to come at me incorrect totally out of left field.

I had watched fellow Temptation Paul Williams deteriorate by pickling his liver right before my face. I tried to help, but that task played like a one-man band. Otis had always gone above and beyond the call of duty to demonstrate his propensity for selfishness. But when the O virus managed to infect my best friend Melvin, I was not only disappointed, but I was also hurt. I wanted Melvin to step up to the plate and take a positive position on my behalf. That positive position meant calling what's right, right, and what's wrong—the dirty lowdown that it is.

Sadly, to me, Melvin didn't. Silently, he turned the other way implying it would be in my interest to "be like Jesus." That is, "turn the other cheek" since I was getting paid something. But, the other cheek in this situation was below the belt. That's where I was being kicked, not kissed.

By all means, I have no problem in hearing "a word in season." I just find it amazing that those most willing to speak it are most often clueless with respect to the hearer's weariness.

The song is "God Bless the Child That's Got His Own." But instead of "Lady," it was "Richard Sings the Blues." And that was the tune being sung without a Temptation five-part harmony. I was doing a solo performance. Just like Eddie Kendricks, I was "all by myself." And like David Ruffin, "my whole word ended."

When the guys you hang with turn away and leave you hanging, you get just a little bit of the feeling Jesus must have felt in the hour of his "temptation." Melvin was my Peter. And as far as Otis, you can fill the appropriate name in that blank.

The bottom line is lesson learned. When it comes to money and trust, you'd be wise to treat the latter like a four-letter word beginning with the sixth letter of the alphabet followed by the word you.

There was no explanation for me being treated like a second-class citizen of Hitsville, USA. It was a cheap shot. But again, this is the entertainment business. If you dance to the music, you have to pay the piper. And you don't have to ask your mama to know that's the truth.

Otis didn't care anything about the feelings of others. Unfortunately, his lack of regard doesn't make him unique or leave him out there all alone. The entertainment industry takes pride in the expression "show business." Breaking it down, those who perform are the show. Those who count the money are the business. Not until more of us on the show side of the business wake up and count the beans instead of just merely drinking the coffee, will operating in a company's best interest be what's totally best for the performing artist?

When you are in a singing group, that group is family. Just as you may love your biological sisters and brothers, the same applies when it comes to your group. Of course, the analogy is also applicable to sports. If it's a team approach, it's through thick and thin. You are concerned about your teammates more than you are yourself—at least you are supposed to be.

The leadership skills of your coach and/or captain should always be about fairness to all the players even if it means sacrifice. In baseball, when a homerun hitter lays down a sacrifice bunt, that sacrifice is for the purpose of advancing someone else for the betterment of the team. His bunt is not about the betterment of the individual player. To the contrary, it's about the team. That unselfish sacrifice can either mean win or loss.

With respect to a winning team—be they Patriots, Giants, Heat, or Temptations—do you complain about what's happening if you know you're being treated unfair, and you're the only one who cares?

Concerning my situation with the Tempts, Melvin and others didn't speak up for me for fear of losing their jobs. Remembering from whence we all came, nobody wanted to go back to that place. Unfortunately, everybody other than me was concerned about self. I loved team Tempts like blood brothers. I'd like to think they loved me too. They just loved the almighty dollar a whole lot more. And just like it's written, it's the love of money that's the root of all evil—not the money itself.

Needless, but necessary to say, this hurt real bad. I'd go so far to say I felt hurt far worse than I had been by the love loss of any woman. So I went from the top of the mountain to the valley without a parachute. Psychologically free falling that fast and far can have an emotional effect on your self-esteem.

The contractual actions of Otis caused me to feel that my talent was less than that of the other group members. Even though I was part of a championship team, I didn't feel like I was part of the team.

The moral of the story is that I had foolishly allowed a fool to steal myself identity by lowering my self-esteem. I was a captain, but I allowed the script to be flipped that would cast me in the nut role of water boy.

All was not well in Hitsville, USA, during those personally trying times. If not for my remembrance of my mother's incredible sacrifices as an unsung hero during every phase and stage of my life and times, the challenges would have been too challenging.

If not for the goodness and grace of God, the temptations that came from being a Temptation would have been a cross too heavy to bear down the "street" that I called my very own.

THE HOMECOMING

One of the coolest things about the day in which we now live is the thing we call the Internet. The net has truly made the world a global village; instead of *Motown*, how about *GloTown*. I mean all of our music lives on YouTube for the globe to see and hear from here to eternity.

You can go online and either connect or reconnect. With respect to the net, the only excuse for not knowing what time it is basically is not wanting to know what time it is.

Seriously, there's been a whole lot written about the Temptations as far as the trials and tribulations I talk about in this book. I don't have to rehash what you already know. My only goal, objective, and motive is to give you a perspective on what was the golden era of American music from a "Street" perspective that seemed to transcend every color but the green upon which the images of dead presidents are printed.

We as Temptations fell prey to the power of the Almighty dollar. But with a name like "Temptation," if you don't pray, you will be somebody's prey. In our case, that somebody was more often than not our own selves.

Think about it. The Temptations left Motown for Atlantic Records and then came back to Motown.

Go figure.

We were all so done with NS (I won't use the N- or the S-word in this book). It was simply time to go. After all, the grass is always greener on the other side of the hill. Of course, that's what you think until you get over to the other side of the hill and see for yourself. When you're on top looking down, a lot of times what you think is grass is really just weeds.

And if the baggage you carry to the other side of the hill is the exact same baggage you had on the side from whence you came, well, it ain't rocket science in terms of the equation. Billy Preston was no Albert Einstein, but he got it right when he said, "Nothing from nothing leaves nothing." Atlantic Records might just as well been Pacific Records. The move gave the Temptations nothing compared to what we already had.

Why?

Well, Atlantic Records wanted the Temptations with Dennis Edwards on board. The Temptations had been branded with Dennis out front. When I recommended that Dennis take the place of David Ruffin in 1968, from that point in time to 1976, Dennis was the man. Again, if you don't remember (or weren't born), go online, "stop, look, and listen" to the chart busters that the Temptations rolled out with Dennis Edwards as lead vocalist.

But Otis, for some inexplicable reason that once again even Mr. Spock can't go figure, decides Dennis has now gotten too big for the slacks that Otis wants him to wear.

One more time again, this isn't NASA. Atlantic Records wanted the full Monty. I mean what's an ice cream cone without the ice cream!

When Otis Williams, as the leader of the pack, fired Dennis Edwards because Dennis was getting too much attention (after eight years of getting attention), it is totally illogical (Captain Otis T. Williams) to think moving to a new label (Atlantic) is going to be the starship *Enterprise* to boldly take you where you've gone before. Now I'm talking about two Grammys minimum!

Bottom line, Atlantic wanted Dennis. Atlantic took a chance on the Temptations minus Dennis with the hope that lightning would strike the same tree twice. But it didn't happen. The move to Atlantic was like the *Titanic.*

But when it comes to them there Reflections, Otis fired David Ruffin for cause. And then there was Eddie Kendricks simply leaving—for cause.

Then there was Otis firing Damon Harris for cause too— which could have been written "Cause II" as in the sequel.

Like I said, Motown's style of management when it came to us wasn't NASA; it was just NASTY. Yes, we skyrocketed like astronauts. But we weren't treated like the Temptations; we were treated like the Monkees. We were not on board to manipulate any of the machinery; according to Otis, we were just along for the ride.

Damon was younger than all of us. But Damon, like I said earlier, could sing his young blood butt right off the chain.

Otis really didn't want Damon in the group even though Damon more than proved he could do an Eddie Kendricks as good as Eddie Kendricks. The official reason for Otis's reluctance concerning Damon was based on Damon being about ten years everybody else's junior. The unofficial reason, however, was the fact that Damon was a brash, confident young brotha who wasn't going to stroke your ego to either get a job or keep one.

The mere fact that Damon waltzed up to me in the wings of a DC venue claiming he had the "right stuff" spoke volumes about the Damon Harris brand of character.

And the fact that Damon delivered to the tune of a Temptations' second Grammy for "Papa Was a Rollin' Stone" establishes him for who and for way much more than he claimed to be only one year earlier.

So, no; it wasn't surprising that Otis had a problem with Damon Harris similar to the problem he had with David, Eddie, and Dennis. And guess what? Just as Paul shared his last name with Otis, Damon shared his first name with Otis. Damon was born Otis Robert Harris. Damon dropped the "Otis" in an attempt to avoid that "ball of confusion."

Unfortunately, changing the name didn't change the game. The Otis Williams problem with personnel remained the same when you get right down to the real nitty-gritty.

Strictly because Damon Harris wasn't going to kiss anybody's rear end, he was gone in a streaking comet's flash. But young blood didn't crash and burn on the dark side of the moon. Damon just didn't get invited to the Christmas party called the 1982 Temptations Reunion Tour.

Bottom line again, however, the party was over that same year anyway. Otis fired David Ruffin and Eddie Kendricks shortly after Christmas. Motown's homecoming featuring the *Return of the Magnificent Seven* minus Damon Harris was very short-lived.

Let's put the real in it. The entertainment business is dominated by strong personalities. If you don't have a strong personality characterized by a big ego, chances are you're not going to thrive even if you manage to survive. The "fabulous five who evolved into the *Magnificent Seven* were characterized by very strong and confident personalities. We were, and for those who haven't turned in their bucket list, still are professional entertainers.

Anyone who is going to be up in the mix when it comes to strong, confident personalities is going to have to be self-secure in who they are first. And self-security means knowing who you are first before taking steps to deal beyond yourself.

A true leader has the unique, God-given ability to get the best out of those he or she is around. An effective leader can't be intimidated by the success of those in his or her camp. When the goal is success, if the soldiers are looking good so will be the lieutenants, captains, majors, colonels, and generals. The whole entire army.

The very bottom line in this or any business is this: lead, follow, or get out of the way.

We, as Temptations, as a group, needed ego management. Giving Otis the benefit of the doubt, maybe he did the best he could. But when doing the best you can is your only excuse for not being all you can be, is that "best efforts" method behind the madness really good enough to excuse you from the mess you've made?

Is it really all good to reminisce about the millions made in record sales when your reminiscing is being done from a two bedroom flat that's being paid by a fixed income monthly check? Or the legacy you leave your wife, significant other, and children is little more than a footnote found when your name is Googled?

While it's great that all of us will live long on YouTube from here and now to eternity, economic prosperity is not a measure of how many hits your webpage gets if you ain't the one getting paid. Putting the real in it, is the ability to say my daddy sang "Papa Was a Rollin' Stone" all that different from your daddy being a rollin' stone if all he left you was alone?

I was told that somewhere in the world that a Temptations tune is being played once every thirteen-point-five (13.5) seconds. Now, I don't know who figured that out. But I'm certain whoever did was enrolled at the University of ASCAP, or BMI.

By Temptations tune, I'm talking not only the songs we physically sung, but those that were sung and sampled in some way, shape, and form by others. And you don't have to be a genius to figure out if you add some Sly Stone everyday people to the equation who are just singing in the shower, that 13.5 probably drops to every five seconds!

In case you don't know, ASCAP and BMI are all about the Benjamins. While those two giants are there to make sure folks get paid, the folks getting fat in our case were not the ones who were the real reason causing folks to buy the records.

Remove Eddie Kendricks's voice from the lead on "The Girl's Alright with Me" and "Just My Imagination." Would you still buy the song, dance, and hum along? Same applies to songs with the voice of David Ruffin out front. Face it, "My Girl" minus David is orange juice minus the oranges. And the same holds true with Paul Williams, Melvin Franklin, Dennis Edwards, Damon Harris, and yours truly. All of us who had the pleasure and privilege of being out front or soloing on a Temptations' hit tune, unfortunately, were played like pawns instead of knights on the Motown management chessboard.

With the addition of Otis Williams, you can't take five guys from humble backgrounds, cast them in the roles of American idols, and then expect them to deal with fame, fortune, and all that jazz like it was a stroll in the park. Those five guys are spiritually blessed, but they'll be socially lucky to end up owning a Five Guys burger stand at the end of the day. Or, just let me say, all of us, with the exception of Otis, couldn't afford to buy a Five Guys burger stand at the end of the day.

So, you go figure. We already have.

Even though "mama said there would be days like this," those days could have been better for us all if the selfish need for greed, and to be all that at the expense of all others hadn't been the dominating spiritual force. Firing and hiring; being sly, slick, and wicked; smiling faces pretending to be your friend—these were and are the "temptations" that many of us Temptations were led into by the Gospel according to Motown, as preached by those who were managerially ordained.

After leaving Atlantic to come back home to Motown, Dennis Edwards was rehired by Otis Williams, and then fired again by Otis, then rehired again by Otis only to be fired a third time by Otis. One day, maybe Dennis Edwards will tell the story that I know he has to tell.

The unceremonious departures of David Ruffin, Eddie Kendricks, Dennis Edwards, and Damon Harris were prompted by spite. Despite all that those four men contributed to the Motown sound and the millions of dollars that Motown made directly off of their skills, they were used, abused, and kicked to the curb with the grace that's employed in kicking an empty can.

With the departures of David, Eddie, Dennis, and Damon, a bright and shining star came shooting through our life space by the name of Ali-Ollie Woodson. Ollie's voice out front on the 1984 smash hit "Treat Her Like a Lady" gave us our first chart buster since the mid-'70s.

Unfortunately, Ollie was fired by Otis in 1987 and replaced by Dennis. But even though Ollie came back home when Otis fired Dennis for the third and last time, Ollie had still suffered the same fate as all of his lead vocal Temptations predecessors.

Now how do you think Donald Trump would analyze this sort of corporate managerial shenanigans? How far do you think the big O would get as the Donald's apprentice?

I don't know about you, but I think Otis would have gotten the DTs before the third show of his appearance!

How humiliating is it to be hired and fired on a whim?

But how sad to need a job so bad, that you are willing to put up with kiss-ass humiliation in order to survive.

Check out the lyrics to our 1973 top 10 hit "Masterpiece":

> Where I was born everything was dull and dingy
> I lived in a place they called "The Inner City"
> Getting ahead was strictly a no no
> 'Cause nobody cares what happens to the folks
> That live in the ghetto
> Thousands of lives wasting away
> People living from day to day
> It's a challenge just staying alive
> 'Cause in the ghetto only the strong survive.
> Money I ain't got none, job can't find one
> The streets raised me from a baby,
> Thousands of lives wasting away
> People living from day to day
> It's a challenge just staying alive

'Cause in the ghetto only the strong survive
Broken down homes, kids strung out
They don't even know what life's all about
Stealin' cars, robbin' bars
Mugging, drugs, rat infested
And no one's interested
Kids dodging cars for recreation
Only adds to a mother's frustration
Break-ins, folks comin' home
And finding all their possessions gone
Oh it's an ev'ry day thing—in the ghetto.

Again, it's important to understand that we not only sang these songs, but we also felt them. And we felt them because we lived them!

So, ask yourself, why did we take so much crap off of Otis as an instrument of Berry Gordy's machine called Motown? Well, the words of that "masterpiece" are an explanation.

Our voices, looks, and talent, along with our individual and collective swag as Temptations, had given us an escape from the self-degradation that usually comes with poverty. None of us wanted to go back to where we first belonged. So some of us were willing to accept a form of self-degradation that was considered the lesser of two evils. Dealing with Otis and Motown was better than "comin' home" and finding what little you individually had gone.

As Smokey seconded that emotion with the classic line "a taste of honey's worse than none at all," consider the fact that we had played to the princes and the paupers. We had done every major city in America, including those in Europe, Asia, and Africa. As far as we know, presidents and their first ladies had "boogied on down" to a Temptations' song at some time or another.

Keeping it real, driving a bus, working at the post office, or being a middle manager at Wal-Mart, K-Mart, Target, or Dollar

General just isn't going to scratch that itch to do what you've done, if you've done anything like we as the Temptations were doing.

Otis Williams, Shelley Berger, and all in the Motown management family knew once you are hooked on phonics, as in making music, eating at Sonics will no longer do it for you. You are a certified junkie for the rest of your life. As a matter of fact, for most of us, what we were doing is all we could do anyway. We had no marketable skills beyond singing as a profession. A lot of us didn't even have high school diplomas. That's why you see the names of the R & B groups you grew up on in the '60s and '70s still out there until the last man standing in the original group dies of old age. Life after Motown for many of us became an annual fund-raiser for PBS. Or a Best of Soul Train, '60s and '70s *TIME-LIFE* infomercial.

Can we as Temptations blame anyone other than ourselves for allowing an Otis or a Shelly take advantage of us? The keeping it real answer, of course, is no. We had a choice in the matter. Nobody told us to spend all of the little money we made on cars, clothes, jewelry, fine women, and wine. Individually and collectively we could have spent a little something on a qualified entertainment attorney that would have advised us individually and collectively with regard to our best interest.

We didn't realize that not being able to understand the fine print on our individual contracts would one day find us "depressed and down-hearted" just like one of the Temptations' songs we were singing.

Since most of us didn't turn to an attorney, what was turned to was cloud nine. Essentially, that means our only legacy is the knowledge that we were members of one of the greatest singing groups that ever was, or will ever be.

So this book is only about my life as a member of the Temptations. It's not about my life beyond the Temptations.

During the course of my twenty-two-year stay with the Tempts, we had close to fifty top-40 hits on Billboard's R & B chart. Now, I don't bring that up to throw roses or kudos at myself. I just say that to quiz this. Just how many hits would we have had if the "ball" had stayed a red carpet event? Just what would we have accomplished if the yellow brick road hadn't wound its way through a tree-lined forest rooted with unbridled egotism, selfishness, and the need to be "all that" you really aren't?

What if the "ball" hadn't turned "confusing?"

Right before leaving the Tempts, I met my current wife Cindy. I believe meeting Cindy was God's way of telling me it's time to go with respect to the Temptations. God always gives us something to have and to hold when it's time to "give it up, turn it loose." I had been holding on to "the temptations" physically and literally for dear life. Instead of the Temptations, Cindy is my dear and my life. God willing, she will be till the day I die.

I left the Temptations in 1993. It's been twenty years at the writing of this book. There is more I could have said about my departure. There is more I could have said about my life as a Temptation. The story here, however, is more about the *we* than it is about the me.

David Ruffin, Eddie Kendricks, Paul Williams, and Melvin Franklin were my friends. They were my brothers first and foremost. I was with them in the beginning. I was with them until the end.

We had an agreement that whichever one of us God chose to be the "last man standing" that one remaining would tell the true story about the Temptin' Temptations.

The true story wouldn't be a fairy tale to make anyone of us larger in death than we were in life. It wouldn't be a story fluffed or puffed to build anyone of us up at the expense of tearing anyone of us down. We agreed to simply tell it like it t-i-s is.

You see, when all is said, sung, and done, all that remains to sum it all up is that hyphen that separates the year you were born from that year you die. I guess in the final analysis, it's really not all about the Benjamins; it's all about the "hyphen." What we do between the space separating our birth and death is the life God gives us to do our thing. We did our thing. As brothers, we did it better than the Isleys could ever sing it.

And as brothas, it was our hope that all who read what is written by whichever one of us did the writing, the reader will realize a coin not only has two sides, but it also has an edge. The Temptations I've written about on the pages of this book were not only "standing on the top," but we were also standing on the edge.

I hope my perspective will both put and keep the real in it. After all, "that's what the world is today" just like it was then.